D1084293

ASPECTS OF NARRATIVE

ASPECTS OF NARRATIVE

Selected Papers from the ENGLISH INSTITUTE

EDITED WITH A FOREWORD BY *J. Hillis Miller*

Columbia University Press

NEW YORK AND LONDON 1971

Acknowledgment is made to E. P. Dutton & Co., Inc., for permission to print the essay "Witness and Testament: Two Contemporary Classics" by Warner Berthoff, which appears in the book *Fictions and Events* by Warner Berthoff, published by E. P. Dutton & Co., Inc. (copyright © 1971 by Warner Berthoff).

FOREWORD

The essays in this volume were presented at three conferences of the English Institute. The first four papers were read in 1970 at the conference on "The Study of Narrative Techniques in Contemporary European and American Criticism," directed by Professor Paul De Man. The essay by Professor Leo Bersani was read in 1969 at the conference on "The Confessional Mode: Revealing and Concealing," directed by Professor Norman N. Holland, and the last two papers were read in 1970 at the conference on "The Personal Mode in American Literature," directed by Professor J. C. Levenson. Though no attempt was made to impose a foolish consistency of approach or theme on these conferences, a concern for the interpretation of narrative runs through the seven essays.

This region of criticism is in fact especially active just now. New ways of approaching narrative or old ways dressed anew are being developed in many countries and for many literatures. A new sense of the subtlety and flexibility required for the criticism of fiction is emerging. The essays presented here constitute a constellation of points, or the tips of several icebergs, indicating, however incompletely, the present state of the interpretation of narrative in several countries. It may be hoped that putting them side by side in this way will encourage interaction among groups which have sometimes remained parochial, self-enclosed, working toward insights which are being reached independently by a different route in another country. The essayists take their examples from almost the whole range of English fiction, from Tolstoy, from Proust, and from the admirable sequence of American autobiographies leading from Franklin to Malcolm X and Norman Mailer, but the focus remains to a considerable degree methodological. What distinguishes prose narrative from other forms of literature? How can it be talked about intelligently? What kinds does it have?

The answers suggested for such questions in the several essays may stand alone, but each essay in fact grows out of a more or less fully developed local context of criticism. Wolfgang Iser's paper is an example of a provocative investigation by certain German critics of the role of the reader in the complex interaction involving author, narrator, characters, and reader in the creation of meaning in a narrative. This interest Professor Iser shares with his colleagues in literature at the Universität Konstanz, Hans Robert Jauss and others. Gérard Genette's essay is one version of the scrupulous analysis of linguistic details and details of structure one finds in much contemporary French criticism of fiction. This approach has been stimulated in part by the renewal of interest in the older work of the Russian formalists, in part by the impact of linguistic or anthropological "structuralism," and in part by the recent challenging revival of rhetoric by such critics as Roland Barthes. An indication of the special importance which the analysis of narrative has at the moment for these critics is the fact that the Winter, 1970, issue of the new journal *Poétique*, edited by M. Genette, Hélène Cixous, and Tzvetan Todorov, is almost entirely concerned not with "poetry" or "poetics" in the usual sense but with various problems in the interpretation of narrative. The same special value given to criticism of fiction may also be observed in other French critical periodicals, for example in *Tel Quel* or in *Communications*.

The essays by American critics included here suggest that there may be a turning away, in current work, from our traditional concern for "point of view," with its overt or covert commitment to certain representationalist assumptions. This turning away takes a variety of forms. There may be a new interest in the way a narrative is a product of a desire on the part of its author to create a supplementary reality, or in the way a narrative may be an incomplete structure creating its own meaning, or in the function in a narrative of details which are "loose ends," apparently "irrelevant" in the sense that they cannot easily be incorporated into some neat pattern of interrelated meanings. In this country as in Europe new scrutiny is also being given to forms of narrative, like autobiography, which do not fit the traditional rubrics of the criticism of fiction, forms which may be not so much the copy of a preexisting reality as a progressive act of self-creation or at any rate of self-extension. Present in all the essays, in fact, is one form or another of the opposition, fundamental in literature, between mimetic realism and some conception of a narrative as a fabric of language generating meaning from the reference of words to other, anterior words.

J. HILLIS MILLER

The Johns Hopkins University
January, 1971

CONTENTS

FOREWORD V
J. Hillis Miller *The Johns Hopkins University*

INDETERMINACY AND THE READER'S
RESPONSE IN PROSE FICTION I
Wolfgang Iser *Universität Konstanz*

MOLESTATION AND AUTHORITY
IN NARRATIVE FICTION 47
Edward W. Said *Columbia University*

THE IRRELEVANT DETAIL
AND THE EMERGENCE OF FORM 69
Martin Price *Yale University*

TIME AND NARRATIVE IN
A la recherche du temps perdu 93
Gérard Genette *Ecole des hautes études, Paris*

PROUST AND THE ART OF INCOMPLETION 119
Leo Bersani *Rutgers University*

AUTOBIOGRAPHY AND AMERICA   143
    James M. Cox   *Dartmouth College*

WITNESS AND TESTAMENT:
TWO CONTEMPORARY CLASSICS   173
    Warner Berthoff   *Harvard University*

THE ENGLISH INSTITUTE, 1970   199

PROGRAM   201

REGISTRANTS   205

ASPECTS OF NARRATIVE

 Wolfgang Iser

INDETERMINACY AND THE READER'S
RESPONSE IN PROSE FICTION

I

"In place of a hermeneutics we need an erotics of art." [1] With
this irony-edged demand Susan Sontag, in her essay "Against
Interpretation," aimed at that form of textual interpretation
which is concerned with finding out the meaning contained in
literary texts. What was originally a useful activity—the
process whereby damaged texts were made legible, or intelligible, that is, by supplying meaning to the damaged parts—
has, according to Susan Sontag, mushroomed more and more
into a distrust of the perceptible form of the text, whose so-
called hidden meaning supposedly can only be revealed
through interpretation. [2] That texts have contents, which in
turn are carriers of meaning, was until the arrival of modern
art an almost uncontested assumption. Therefore interpretation

[1] Susan Sontag, *Against Interpretation and Other Essays* (New
York, 1966), p. 14.

[2] *Ibid.*, pp. 6 f.

was always legitimate if it reduced the text to meaning. The advantage of this was that meanings could be generalized, that they represented established conventions, and that they brought out accepted or at least understandable values. Interpretation served the purpose of conveying meaning, in order that comprehension might be assured. Texts had to be seen in the context of what was already familiar or comprehensible to the reader. The zeal of critics for classification—their passion for pigeonholing, one might almost call it—only subsided when some special significance of the content had been discovered and its value ratified by means of what was already common knowledge. Referral of the text to some already existing frame of reference became an essential aim of this method of interpretation, by means of which the sharpness of a text was inevitably dulled.

But how shall we then describe the dynamic character of a text? Can one, in fact, assess the keen disturbance so often experienced in reading serious literature? Some texts certainly have stimulating moments that disturb and even provoke a certain nervousness in the reader—a reaction that Susan Sontag might describe as having to do with the "erotics of art." If texts actually possessed only the meaning brought to light by interpretation, then there would remain very little else for the reader. He could only accept or reject it, take it or leave it. The fundamental question is, however, what actually does take place between text and reader? Is it possible to look into that relationship at all, or is not the critic simply plunging into a private world where he can only make vague conjectures and speculations? Is one able to express anything at all about those highly heterogeneous reactions that run between text and reader? At the same time it must be pointed out that a text can only come to life when it is read, and if it is to be examined, it must therefore be studied through the eyes of the reader. "Involvement of the reader or spectator as accomplices or collaborators is essential in the curious situation of artistic communication."[3] What, then, does the process of reading consist of?

Briefly, it might be described as the reader's transformation of signals sent out by the text. But if the act of reading is indeed the transformation of the author's signals, then one is bound to ask whether such a process can ever be described without recourse to the psychology of the reader. Then again, if one tries to draw a distinction between a text and the various possible forms of its transformation, one risks being accused of denying the identity of a text and of merely letting it dissolve into the arbitrariness of subjective perception. A text, the argument runs, must represent something, and the meaning of what is represented exists independently of every single reaction that such a meaning might arouse. To counter this, however, one might suggest that this "meaning," which is apparently independent of every realization of the text, is in itself nothing more than an individual reading experience which has now simply been identified with the text itself. Interpretations based on conveying meaning have always been along these lines, with a consequent dilution of the texts they dealt with. Fortunately, such interpretations have been contradicted from time to time, for the most part, however, only with the consequence that an equally restricted interpretation was ultimately set up in place of the one knocked down. The history of re-

[3] Lowry Nelson, Jr., "The Fictive Reader and Literary Self-Reflexiveness," in *The Disciplines of Criticism: Essays in Literary Theory, Interpretation, and History*, Honoring René Wellek on the Occasion of his Sixty-fifth Birthday, ed. Peter Demetz, Thomas Greene, and Lowry Nelson, Jr. (New Haven, 1968), p. 174.

sponses to literary works, which in turn is a history of variations, offers countless examples of this.

If it were really true—as the author of a certain well-known essay on "the Art of Interpretation" would have us believe—that the meaning is concealed within a text itself, one cannot help wondering why texts should indulge in such a "hide-and-seek" with their interpreters; and even more puzzling, why the meaning, once it has been found, should then change again, even though the letters, words, and sentences of the text remain the same. Isn't it here that the meaning-grinder begins to obscure the text, thus canceling out his own avowed intent—to bring clarity and light to the text he is examining?

Shouldn't the interpreter in fact renounce his sanctified role of conveying meanings, if he wants to open up the possibilities of a text? His description of the text is, after all, nothing more than an experience of a cultured reader—in other words, it is only one of the possible realizations of a text. If this is the case, we could then maintain—at least tentatively—that meanings in literary texts are mainly generated in the act of reading; they are the product of a rather difficult interaction between text and reader and not qualities hidden in the text, the tracing out of which remains reserved alone for that traditional kind of interpretation I have described. If the individual reader generates the meaning of a text, then it follows that these meanings will always appear with a slightly individualistic touch.

There are many more questions one could ask of "the Art of Interpretation," but the nature of the problem is already tangible and can now be stated: If a literary text could really be reduced to one particular meaning, it would be the expression of something else—namely, of that meaning the status of which is determined by the fact that it exists independently of the text. Put in extreme terms this means that the literary text would then be the illustration of this meaning existing outside itself. Thus the literary text would sometimes be read as evidence of the *Zeitgeist*, sometimes as an expression of its author's neuroses, sometimes as a mirror-reflection of social conditions, or what have you.

Of course, no one will deny that literary texts do contain a historical substratum, but the manner in which literature takes it up and communicates it does not seem to be determined by merely historical circumstances, but by the specific aesthetic structure inherent in it. That is why we often have the feeling, when reading works of past ages, that we are actually transported back into those times and moving in historical circumstances as if we belonged to them or as if the past were again the present. The preconditions for this experience are certainly provided by the text, but we as readers also play a part in the creation of this impression. It is we who bring the text to life. Obviously, the text must offer a certain amount of latitude, as far as its realization is concerned, for different readers at different times have always had differing apprehensions of such texts, even though the general impression may be the same— that the world revealed, however far back in the past it may lie, comes alive in the present.

At this point we can formulate our task in more precise terms: How can we describe the relationship between text and reader? We shall search for the answer in three stages. The first step is to indicate the special qualities of a literary text that distinguish it from other kinds of text. The second step will be to name and analyze the basic elements of the cause of the response to literary works. Here we shall pay special attention to different degrees of what I should like to call indeterminacy in a text and the various ways in which it is brought about. In a third step we must attempt to clarify the observable increase of indeterminacy in narrative literature since the eighteenth century. If one supposes that indeterminacy embodies an elementary condition for readers' reactions, then one must ask what its expansion, above all in modern literature, indicates. It changes without doubt the relationship between text and reader. The more texts lose their determinacy, the more strongly is the reader shifted into the full operation of their possible intentions. If indeterminacy exceeds a certain toleration limit, the reader will feel strained to an almost intolerable degree. He can in that case reveal attitudes which might lead to a rather surprising insight into what usually determines his reactions. At this point, the question arises as to what insights into the workings of the human mind literature can open up. To raise this question means at the same time to conceive the relation between text and reader as a starting point for a more thoroughgoing investigation of the connection between literature and consciousness.

II

Let us come to our first step. How can we describe the status of a literary text? The first point is that it differs from any other text that presents an object which exists independent of the text. If a piece of writing describes an object that exists with equal determinacy outside it, then the text is simply an exposition of the object. In Austin's terms, it is a "constative utterance," as opposed to a "performative utterance," [4] which actually creates its object. It goes without saying that literary

---

[4] J. L. Austin, *How to Do Things with Words*, ed. J. O. Urmson (Cambridge, Mass., 1962), pp. 1 ff.

texts belong to the second category. There is no concrete object corresponding to them in the real world, although of course they constitute their objects out of elements to be found in the real world.

This rough distinction of texts as statement and performance must, however, be still further differentiated in order to arrive at a preliminary definition of a literary text. For there are texts that constitute something without being literary. For instance, all texts which present claims, state aims, define purposes, and formulate rules likewise produce new objects, but these objects achieve their existence only through the determinacy brought about by the text. Legal texts are the most obvious examples of this form of language. They lay down principles that are binding for the behavior of human beings. A literary text, however, can never set out anything factual of this nature. It is not surprising, therefore, that we call such a text fiction, for fiction—in its simplest definition—is form without reality.

But is literature wholly devoid of reality, or is it perhaps imbued with a reality of its own, which sets it off from the linguistics of expository texts as well as from those texts which constitute general norms of human behavior? A literary text neither portrays nor creates objects in the way we have described; at best we can say that it is the description of reactions to objects.[5] "All art originates," E. H. Gombrich once remarked, "in our reactions to the world rather than in the visible world itself." [6] This is why we recognize in literature so many elements that play a part in our own experience. They

[5] This matter is also treated in Susanne K. Langer's *Feeling and Form* (New York, 1953), p. 59: "The solution of the difficulty lies, I think, in the recognition that what art expresses is *not* actual feeling, but ideas of feeling; as language does not express actual things and events but ideas of them."

[6] E. H. Gombrich, *Art and Illusion* (London, 1962), p. 76.

are simply put together in a different way—in other words, they constitute a familiar world reproduced in an unfamiliar form. Thus the intention of a literary text can never be completely identified with our experience. Instead, it presents reactions to and attitudes toward the real world, and it is these reactions and attitudes that constitute the reality of a literary text. If a literary text presents no real objects, it nevertheless establishes its reality by the reader's participation and by the reader's response. The reader, however, cannot refer to any definite object or independent facts in order to judge whether the text has presented its subject rightly or wrongly. This possibility of verification that all expository texts offer is, precisely, denied by the literary text. At this point there arises a certain amount of indeterminacy which is peculiar to all literary texts, for they permit no referral to any identical real-life situation.

When the reader has gone through the various perspectives offered him by the text, he is left with nothing but his own experience to judge what has been communicated to him. There are two extremes of reaction that can arise from the confrontation between one's own world and that of the literary work involved: either the literary world seems fantastic, because it contradicts our own experience, or it seems trivial, because it merely echoes our own. This shows clearly the significance of our own experience in the realization of a text, and here we have an initial insight into the specific nature of a literary text. Firstly, it differs from other forms of writing in that it neither describes nor constitutes real objects; secondly, it diverges from the real experiences of the reader in that it offers views and opens up perspectives in which the empirically known world of one's own personal experience appears changed. And so the literary text cannot be fully identified either with the real objects of the outside world or with the experiences of the reader.

This lack of identification produces a degree of indeterminacy which normally the reader will counterbalance by the act of reading. Here, too, there is scope for a wide variety of reactions on the part of the reader. The gaps of indeterminacy can be filled in by referring the text to real, verifiable factors, in such a way that it appears to be nothing more than a mirror-reflection of these factors. In this case it loses its literary quality in the reflection. Alternatively, the indeterminacy of a text may be so resistant to counterbalancing that any identification with the real world is impossible. Then the world of the text establishes itself as being in competition with the familiar world, a competition which must inevitably have some repercussions on the familiar one. In this case, the text may tend to function as a criticism of life.

Indeterminacy can also be counterbalanced at any given time in terms of the individual experience of the reader. He can reduce a text to the level of his own experiences, provided that he projects his own standards onto the text in order to grasp its specific meaning. This, too, is a counterbalancing of indeterminacy which disappears when the subjective norms of the reader guide him through the text. On the other hand, a text may conceivably contradict our own preconceptions to such a degree that it calls forth drastic reactions, such as throwing a book away or, at the other extreme, being compelled to revise those preconceptions. This also constitutes a way of removing indeterminacy which always permits the possibility of connecting one's own experience with what the text wants to convey. Whenever this happens, indeterminacy tends to disappear, because communication has occurred.

Such basic reactions clarify the status of the literary text: Its main characteristic is its peculiar halfway position between the world of real objects and the reader's own world of experience. The act of reading is therefore a process of seeking to pin down the oscillating structure of the text to some specific meaning.

III

So far, we have only described the literary text, as it were, from the outside. We must now, in a second step, mention certain important formal conditions which give rise to indeterminacy in the text itself. At once, we are confronted with the question as to what really is the substance of such a text, for it has no counterpart in the world of empirical objects. The answer is that literary objects come into being through the unfolding of a variety of views which constitute the "object" in stages and at the same time give a concrete form for the reader to contemplate. We shall call such views "schematized views," [7] following a term coined by the Polish philosopher Roman Ingarden, because every one of them sets out to present the object not in an incidental or even accidental way, but in a representative manner. How many of these views are necessary to give a clear idea of the literary object? Obviously, a large number, if one is to get a precise conception.

This raises a highly relevant problem: each single view will generally reveal only one representative aspect. It therefore determines the literary object, and at the same time it raises the need for a new determination. This means that a literary object never reaches the end of its many-faceted determinacy. In

[7] See Roman Ingarden, *Das literarische Kunstwerk* (Tübingen, 1960), pp. 261 ff.

other words, a literary object can never be given final definition. This is borne out, for example, by the endings of many novels which often resemble a *tour de force* simply because the book must come to an end. Indeterminacy is then counterbalanced by the author himself with an ideological or utopian solution. There are other novels, though, which articulate this inconclusiveness at the end.

If we assume that the "schematized views" form a basic characteristic of the literary text, nothing has thus far been said as to how they link up with one another. While they touch upon one another, the degree of connections is usually not stated, but has to be inferred. The sequence of views has the appearance of being dissevered here and there, resembling a cutting technique. The most frequent application of this technique occurs where several plot threads run simultaneously, but must be dealt with one after the other. The connections which develop among such views are, as a rule, not set out by the text itself, although the way in which they are related is important for the intention of the text. In other words, between the "schematized views" there is a no-man's-land of indeterminacy, which results precisely from the determinacy of the sequence of each individual view. Gaps are bound to open up, and offer a free play of interpretation for the specific way in which the various views can be connected with one another. These gaps give the reader a chance to build his own bridges, relating the different aspects of the object which have thus far been revealed to him. It is quite impossible for the text itself to fill in the gaps. In fact, the more a text tries to be precise (i.e., the more "schematized views" it offers), the greater will be the number of gaps between the views. Classic examples of this are the last novels of Joyce, *Ulysses* and *Finnegans*

Wake, where the overprecision of the presentation gives rise to a proportionate increase in indeterminacy. We shall return to this point later.

The indeterminate sections or gaps of literary texts are in no way to be regarded as a defect; on the contrary, they are a basic element for the aesthetic response. Generally, the reader will not even be aware of such gaps—at least so far as novels up to the end of the nineteenth century are concerned. Nevertheless, they are not without influence on his reading, for the "schematized views" are continually connected with each other in the reading process. This means that the reader fills in the remaining gaps. He removes them by a free play of meaning-projection and thus by himself repairs the unformulated connections between the particular views. This is borne out by the fact that a second reading of a piece of literature often produces a different impression from the first. The reasons for this may lie in the reader's own change of circumstances, but all the same, the text must be such as to permit of this variation. On a second reading, one has considerably more knowledge about the text, especially if the first reading was only a short time ago. This additional information will affect and condition the meaning-projection, so that now the gaps between the different segments as well as the spectrum of their possible connections, or repair, can be applied in a different or perhaps more intensive way. The increased information that now overshadows the text provides possibilities of combination which were obscured in the first reading. Familiar occurrences now tend to appear in a new light and seem to be at times corrected, at times enriched. But for all that, nothing is formulated in the text itself; rather, the reader himself produces these innovative readings. This would, of course, be impossible if the text itself was not, to some degree, indeterminate, leaving room for the change of vision.[8]

In this way, every literary text invites some form of participation on the part of the reader. A text which lays things out

[8] At this point there ought to follow a critical discussion of the term "Unbestimmtheitsstellen" (gaps of indeterminacy), which Ingarden sometimes uses in his writings about the work of art, in order to differentiate clearly the concept of this essay from an apparently related posing of the problem. Such a discussion would, however, exceed the limits of an essay and would certainly upset its balance. It will be dealt with later in a more detailed presentation. However, a few important differences might be stated here. Ingarden employs the concept of "Unbestimmtheitsstellen" to indicate, above all, the distinction between literary objects and real ones. Hence the "Unbestimmtheitsstellen" reveal what the subject of literature or the literary object respectively lacks in comparison to the total definitiveness of real things. Accordingly, one of the main operations going on in a literary work is the constant removal of "Unbestimmtheitsstellen" in the act of composition, thus diminishing their occurrences as far as possible. Thereby the latent deficiency adhering to them can clearly be seen. Yet the gaps of indeterminacy are vital for eliciting the reader's response and are consequently an important factor for the effect exercised by a work of art.

For Ingarden, however, this function plays hardly any role at all, as can be seen in his book *Vom Erkennen des literarischen Kunstwerks* (Tübingen, 1968), in which the conditions of the literary response are analyzed. Communication occurs, in Ingarden's terms, whenever the reader feels the impact of the "Ursprungsemotion" (original emotion) radiating from the literary text, so that the explanation of responses is nothing but a rehearsal of the well-known arguments of empathy. Consequently, the "Unbestimmtheitsstellen" are defined as the omission of the unimportant, mostly supplementary, details, for which Ingarden often gives quite trivial examples (cf. p. 49). In his opinion there is no compelling necessity for filling in the "Unbestimmtheitsstellen." Occasionally, they may disturb the artistic worth or value—even destroy or annihilate the work of art when, as in modern texts, they increase. Thus for Ingarden the "Unbestimmtheitsstellen" demand before the reader in such a way that he can either accept or reject them will lessen the degree of participation as it allows him nothing but a yes or no. Texts with such minimal indeterminacy tend to be tedious, for it is only when the reader is given the chance to participate actively that he will regard the text, whose intention he himself has helped to compose, as real. For we generally tend to regard things that we have made ourselves as being real. And so it can be said that indeterminacy is the fundamental precondition for reader participation.

We might illustrate this fact by observing one literary form that makes very special use of the technique of indeterminacy. This is the serial story, the text of which is delivered to the reader in carefully measured doses. When serialized novels appear in newspapers today—as is customary in Europe—advertising plays an important role for this kind of publication: the novel has to be introduced in order to attract an audience to it. In the nineteenth century this intention stood completely in the foreground of interest. The great realistic writers courted an audience for their novels by this manner of publication, and it was in this way that many of their most im-

---

only a single activity from the reader—that of completion. This means that the filling in of the "Unbestimmtheitsstellen" contributes toward a completion of the polyphonic harmony, which, for Ingarden, embodies the basic quality of a work of art. If the completion is specified as a supplement of what is omitted, the undynamic quality becomes visible. Moreover, the ideal of polyphonic harmony which Ingarden sets up as a yardstick for judging a work of art lends itself as a means to separate true from false supplementations, and thereby confirms or corrects, respectively, the supplementation the reader is supposed to provide. Behind such a concept there looms the classical conception of a work of art, so that consequently for Ingarden there are true and false realizations of a literary text.

portant works appeared.[9] Charles Dickens actually wrote his
novels from week to week, and in between episodes he tried to
find out as much as possible about the way in which his readers visualized the development of the story.[10]

The experience of the reading public of the nineteenth century is extremely revealing and highly relevant to our discussion: readers often preferred the novel read by installments to
the identical text in book form.[11] The same thing can still be

[9] See Kathleen Tillotson, *Novels of the Eighteen-Forties* (Oxford,
1962), Oxford paperback, pp. 28 ff. and 33, and George H. Ford,
Dickens and His Readers (Princeton, 1955), p. 6.

[10] See Tillotson, *Novels of the Eighteen-Forties*, pp. 34 f. and 36 f.

[11] When Dickens published the first cheap edition of his novels, its
success could hardly be compared with that which the later edi-
tions achieved. The first edition of 1846–47 occurred at a time
during which Dickens still published in serial form; see John Forster, *The Life of Charles Dickens*, Vol. I, ed. A. J. Hoppé (London,
1966), p. 448. In this connection two further examples are instructive for the reader's reactions. *Martin Chuzzlewit*, designated by
Dickens himself as one of his most important novels, proved itself
on its first publication a washout. Forster (*Life*, I, 285) and Ford
(*Dickens and His Readers*, p. 43) are of the opinion that this failure
resulted from the manner of the publication; instead of following
the previous method of weekly installments, this novel appeared
at monthly intervals. The intermissions proved too long. From
Crabb Robinson we know that he found the serial publication of
Dickens's novels so disturbing that he occasionally decided that
he would sooner wait for the book form than endure the anxiety
which the still unforeseeable action produced in him (see Ford, pp.
415 f.). Furthermore, the week-to-week chapters themselves indicate how tightly they were organized with respect to effect. In
book form this manner of composition became so obvious that it
led to critical evaluations by readers (see Ford, pp. 123 f.). On the
specific contact between author and reader in the serialized novel,
see also Tillotson, *Novels of the Eighteen-Forties*, pp. 26 ff. and
33. Trollope was of the opinion that the serialized novel avoided
the "long succession of dull pages" which in the book form could
not be completely bypassed (see Tillotson, p. 40).

seen today, if one only has the patience to go through with the experiment, for most of the stories that appear in papers nowadays tend to belong to the genre we generally call "light literature," bordering on the trivial. The object is still, of course, to attract a large public. If we read such novels in installments, they may at least be bearable; if we read them in book form, generally they will finish us before we finish them.

Let us examine the circumstances underlying this difference. The serialized novel uses a cutting technique. It interrupts the action usually where a certain tension has been built up that demands to be resolved, or where one is anxious to learn the outcome of the events one has just read about. The dramatic interruption or prolongation of suspense is the vital factor that determines the cutting, and the effect is to make the reader try to imagine the continuation of the action. How is it going to go on? In asking this question, we automatically raise the degree of our own participation in the further progress of the action. Dickens was well aware of this fact, that is why he considered his readers to be co-authors.[12]

One could draw up a whole list of such cutting techniques, which for the most part are more sophisticated than the primitive, though highly effective method of suspense. Another way, for instance, of involving the reader in a greater degree of composition is the abrupt introduction of new characters or even new threads of the plot, so that the question arises as to the connections between the story revealed so far and the new, unforeseen situations. This is a matter of discovering links and working out how the narrative will bring the different elements together. In view of the temporary withholding of information, the suggestive effect produced by details will increase, thus again mobilizing a new army of possible solutions.
[12] See Tillotson, *Novels of the Eighteen-Forties*, pp. 25 f.

Such a technique arouses definite expectations which, if the novel is to have any real value, must never be completely fulfilled.

The serialized novel, then, results in a special kind of reading. The interruptions are more deliberate and calculated than those occasioned by random reasons to the reader of a book. In the serialized novel they arise from a strategic purpose. The reader is forced by the pauses imposed on him to imagine more than he could have done if his reading were continuous, and so, if the text of a serialized novel makes a different impression from the text in book form, this is principally because it introduces additional gaps, or alternatively accentuates existing gaps by means of a break until the next installment. This does not mean that its quality is in any way higher. The pauses simply bring out a different kind of realization, in which the reader is compelled to take a more active part by filling in these additional gaps. If a novel *seems* to be better in this form, then this is clear evidence of the importance of indeterminacy in the text-reader relationship. Furthermore, it reveals the requisite degree of freedom which must be guaranteed to the reader in the communication act, so that the message can be adequately received and processed.

At this point there arises another matter which we can only touch upon here. This is the question of the whole repertoire of structures that lead to indeterminacy in a text. Further, we should try to describe the elementary activities in the reading process, of which the reader may not be aware, but which nevertheless operate.

Of the many ways in which a reader's response may be guided, there is one which might serve as a brief illustration for the type of pattern whose function should be investigated. The example is the simplest of all, and therefore the most common one. We all notice in reading novels that the narrative is often interspersed with the author's comments on the events. These comments are frequently in the nature of an evaluation of what has happened. Obviously, the narrative contains elements which require such explanations. In view of our preceding discussion, we might say that here the author himself removes the gaps; for with his comments, he tries to create a uniform conception of his narrative. So long as this remains the sole function of the commentary, the participation of the reader in the execution of the underlying narrative intention must diminish. The author himself tells the reader how his tale is to be understood. At best, the reader can only contradict the author's conception, if he thinks that he can extract different impressions from the work. However, there are many novels which do contain such comments and evaluations, and yet at the same time do not seek to interpret the story from one particular, consistent point of view, but vary considerably as far as perspectives and evaluations are concerned.

This device is already to be discerned at the beginning of the eighteenth century and can be found in many novels whose historical basis is relatively uninteresting for us today. Our pleasure in reading such novels nevertheless does not suffer. In these novels, the author is obviously not exclusively motivated to prescribe, by means of the commenting parts of his text, the understanding of the narrative by the reader. The great English novels of the eighteenth and nineteenth centuries, which today seem just as alive as when written, belong to this category. In these works one has the feeling that the author's remarks are made with a view not to interpreting the meaning of the events but to gaining a position outside them —to regarding them, as it were, from a distance. The commentaries, then, strike one as mere hypotheses, and they seem to imply other possibilities of evaluation than those that arise directly from the events described. This impression is borne out by the fact that the commentaries on different situations often reveal different standpoints of the author himself. Are we, then, to trust the author when he makes his comments? [13] Or are we not, rather, to test what he says for ourselves? Frequently the author's own comments seem to contradict what we have assumed from the events he has described, and if his comments are to make sense to us, we may feel we need further information. Has one perhaps read inattentively there? Or should one, solely on the ground of the reading, correct the comments of the author in order to find by oneself the evaluation of the events? Unexpectedly, then, the reader finds that he is dealing not only with the characters in the novel but also with an author who interposes himself as a mediator between the story and the reader. Now he demands the attention of the reader just as much as the story does itself.

The comments may provoke a variety of reactions. They can disconcert, arouse opposition, charm with contradiction, and frequently uncover many unexpected features of the narrative process, which without these clues one might not have noticed. And so such comments do not provide any definite assessment of the events; rather, they offer an assessment that contains different possibilities open to the reader's choice. Instead of offering the reader a single and consistent perspective, through which he is supposed to look on the events narrated,

[13] Wayne C. Booth, *The Rhetoric of Fiction* (Chicago, 1961), pp. 211 f., differentiates between a "reliable" and an "unreliable narrator," without, however, evaluating this fact for the communication process. The "unreliable narrator" naturally constitutes the more interesting type for the communication process, because his "unreliability" possesses a strategic intention, which relates to the steering of the reader in the text.

the author provides him with a bundle of multiple viewpoints, the center of which is continuously shifted. These comments thus open a certain free play for evaluation, and permit new gaps to arise in the text. They now no longer lie in the re-counted narrative, but between the narrative and the various ways of judging it. They can only be removed, then, while or when judgment is passed on the existing process already de-scribed.

The commentaries provoke the faculty of judgment in two ways: while they exclude any unequivocal judgment of the events, they create gaps which in turn admit many differently shaded judgments; but these judgments are not completely ar-bitrary, because the author outlines by his comments the possi-ble alternatives for the reader. Thus this particular structure involves the reader in the evaluative process and yet, at the same time, it controls the reader's evaluation.

Let us briefly consider this reader-manipulation by an exam-ple which could be considered up to a certain point almost as an embodiment of this process. Given that an author wants to phrase his comments in such a way as not just to limit the scope of his reader's response, but actually to guide him along one specific path, what is he to do? If our observations so far have been correct, we cannot expect the commentary to lay down hard and fast rules for the response desired from the reader. The reader would then merely react to prescriptions laid down, but not in the sense of the planned purpose.

Now the example. It is the well-known passage in Dickens's *Oliver Twist* where the hungry child is in the workhouse and with the courage of despair dares to ask for more gruel. The supervisors of the workhouse are appalled by this monstrous insolence.[14] What does the commentator have to say? Not

[14] See Charles Dickens, *Oliver Twist*, The New Oxford Illustrated Dickens (Oxford, 1959), pp. 12 f.

only does he support them, but he even gives his reasons for doing so.[15] The reaction of the reader is unequivocal, for the author has formulated his commentary in such a way that the reader simply has to reject it. In this manner, the reader's participation in the fate of the child can be brought to the level of actual engagement. The reader is torn from his comfortable seat and plunged into the situation. This is no longer a matter of filling a gap by judging a situation; here the reader is forced to reverse completely a false judgment. If he is to be brought into the action and guided along a specific path, then the text, paradoxically, cannot mean what it says. In this respect Dickens's episode represents an interesting borderline case of indeterminacy. For the same criterion applies here as normally obtains for indeterminacy: what is stated must not exhaust the intention of the text.

Literature abounds in structures like this. Many of them are more complicated than the teamwork between commentator and reader indicated here. One might consider the fact that we as readers are constantly reacting to the characters in a novel, while they never react in any way to our attitudes. In life, obviously, things are very different. What use do we make of the freedom from other people's reactions granted us by the novel? What function has this form of indeterminacy, which elicits our response to the characters, and then seems to leave the rest to us?

At this point we ought to consider above all the technical requirements of language which are responsible for directing the reader's response. We should, in the first place, break down a literary text into its constituent elements, because for an analysis of its appeal it is necessary to know the method according to which it is constructed. If such texts reveal, for example, a cutting—montage—or segmenting technique, it

[15] *Ibid.*, pp. 14 f.

means that they permit relatively great freedom with respect to the concatenation of their textual patterns with one another in the reading process. If, on the other hand, they are structured according to a principle of contrast or opposition, the concatenation of the textual patterns is strongly prescribed. In the one case, a relatively high degree of "performance" is asked of the reader in view of a smaller amount of authorial prescription; in the other case, the opposite is true.

Furthermore, it is important to specify on what textual level and how frequently the gaps occur. If they crop up more often in the narrative strategy and less often in the actions of the characters in the story, different consequences for the communication process will result. Moreover, they are bound to work out quite differently if they occur in the role assigned to the reader.

But the frequency of gaps can also be significant for another kind of classification of textual levels. They may predominate on the syntactic level of the text—that is, in the recognizable system of rules responsible for marshaling the textual patterns into a premeditated order. They may predominate on the pragmatic level of the text—that is, in the intention pursued by it. Or they may ultimately predominate on the semantic level of the text—that is, in the generating of meaning, which is the reader's foremost task. Whatever the distribution of gaps on each of the respective levels, they will have different consequences for the steering process of the reader, the direction of which is to a large extent dependent on the specific textual level in which the gaps predominate. This fact can, however, only be mentioned and not fully discussed here.

IV

Let us now turn to the third stage of our survey: the striking historical fact that since the eighteenth century indeterminacy in literature—or at least an awareness of it—has tended toward a continual increase. The implications of this fact can be illustrated briefly in three examples taken from eighteenth-, nineteenth-, and twentieth-century English literature. There is no doubt that the same phenomena can also be found in the applicable texts of other literatures. The three examples are Fielding's *Joseph Andrews* (1741-42), Thackeray's *Vanity Fair* (1848), and Joyce's *Ulysses* (1922).

Fielding's *Joseph Andrews* began as a parody of Richardson's *Pamela*, in which human nature and conduct were for the most part rigidly fixed. Doubting the definability of human nature, and yet formulating a conception of it—this is the paradoxical starting point of Fielding's novel. The construction is as simple as can be. On the one side is Abraham Adams, the hero, fully equipped with all the virtues of the Enlightenment; on the other side is a reality that ceaselessly attacks these virtues. From the standpoint of the hero, the world seems very bad; from that of the world, the hero is pigheaded and narrow-minded. Now it cannot be the intention of this novel to present the representative of moral principles as a pigheaded individual. At the same time, the world depicted here is no longer set out in accordance with the principles of morality, let alone dominated by them. What is to be discerned is a continual interaction between the two poles of virtue and world, which seems to imply a kind of reciprocal correction. But the nature of this correction is not laid out in the text itself. There is nothing but an interplay of relationships that has long since lost the determinacy recognizable in the two basic positions of hero and reality. This reciprocal correction aims at balancing out, and not at victory or defeat for the one or the other of the parties. Again, the nature of the balance is not set out in the text, but it can be imagined by the reader. Indeed, it may well be that it can only be imagined because it is not set down in words. In acting upon each other, the two sides reveal not so much their actual situation as their potential.

First, the text offers the reader nothing but a collection of positions which it presents in a variety of relationships, without ever formulating the focal point at which they converge. For this point lies in the reader's imagination, and in fact can only be created by his reading. The structure is very close to the reading experience which Northrop Frye has described as follows: "Whenever we read anything, we find our attention moving in two directions at once. One direction is outward and centrifugal, in which we keep going outside our reading, from the individual works to the things they mean, or, in practice, to our memory of the conventional association between them. The other direction is inward or centripetal, in which we try to develop from the words a sense of the larger verbal pattern they make." [16] This "hermeneutic operation" of reading intensifies itself to the degree that the novel renounces definition of its intention. However, the fact that the novel does not set forth its own intention does not mean that no intention exists. Where is it to be found? The answer must be that the reciprocal correction of the positions opens up a dimension which only comes into being through the act of reading. It is only in reading that there occurs an uninterrupted modification of the various positions involved. The hero keeps sallying

[16] Northrop Frye, *Anatomy of Criticism* (New York, 1967), p. 73.

forth into the sordid world of reality, and thus continually provokes changing judgments on the part of the reader. But at the same time, the reader looks through the hero's eyes at the world, so that it, too, is subject to changing judgments. Out of these continually interacting elements, the reader's imagination can build up the pattern of the text—a pattern that varies according to the imagination that is forming it. So the reading becomes an act of generating meaning.

Fielding himself seems to have been fully aware of this construction, for the part that he allocates to the reader is determined by one vital task: the reader is to discover.[17] This demand can be understood historically and structurally. Historically it means that the reader, in discovering that overall pattern for himself, is made to practice one basic principle of the Enlightenment. Structurally it means that the effect of the novel is heightened if it does not provide the focal point of its positions and patterns, but allows the reader himself to remove the inherent indeterminacy.

The author-reader relationship, as developed in the eighteenth-century novel, has been a constant factor in narrative prose and is still in evidence, even though the author seems to have disappeared and the reader to be deliberately excluded from comprehension. While Fielding, referring to his readers, offers them this reassurance: "I am, indeed, set over them for

[17] Henry Fielding, *Joseph Andrews*, Author's Preface, Everyman's Library (London, 1948), p. xxxi: "From the discovery of this affectation arises the Ridiculous, which always strikes the reader with surprise and pleasure; and that in a higher and stronger degree when the affectation arises from hypocrisy, than when from vanity; for to discover any one to be the exact reverse of what he affects, is more surprising, and consequently more ridiculous, than to find him a little deficient in the quality he desires the reputation of." Cf. with this the similar comment in *The History of Tom Jones*, Everyman's Library (London, 1962), p. 12.

their own good only, and was created for their use and not they for mine," [18] Joyce at the other end of the scale drops only the ironic information that the author has withdrawn behind his work, "paring his fingernails." [19] The reader of modern novels is deprived of the assistance which the eighteenth-century writer had given him in a variety of devices, ranging from exhortation to satire and irony. Instead, he is expected to strive for himself to unravel the mysteries of a sometimes strikingly obscure composition. This development reflects the transformation of the very idea of literature, which seems to have ceased to be a means of relaxation and even luxury, making demands now on the capacity of understanding because the world presented seems to have no bearing on what the reader is familiar with. This change did not happen suddenly. The stages of transition are clearly discernible in the nineteenth century, and one of them is virtually a halfway point in the development: the so-called realistic novel, of which Thackeray's *Vanity Fair* is an outstanding example. Here, the author-reader relationship is as different from the eighteenth-century "dialogue" as it is from the twentieth-century demand that the reader find for himself the key to a many-sided puzzle. There is, however, a noticeable increase in indeterminacy in Thackeray, although the author still provides his reader with unmistakable clues to guide him in his search. If indeterminacy regulates the gradual participation of the reader in the fulfillment of the text's intention, one wonders what an intensified participation can involve.

Vanity Fair consists partly of a story, in which are described the social ambitions of two girls in Victorian society, and partly of the commentary by a narrator who introduces him-

[18] Fielding, *Tom Jones*, Vol. I, Book II, 1, p. 39.

[19] James Joyce, *A Portrait of the Artist as a Young Man* (London, 1966), p. 219.

self as a theatrical producer—his productions being almost as
extensive as the story itself. At the start of the novel, the
"Manager of the Performance" [20] gives an outline of what the
audience is to expect. The ideal visitor to "Vanity Fair" is described as a "man with a reflective turn of mind"; [21] this is an
advance indication of what the reader has to accomplish, if he
is to realize the meaning of the proceedings. But at the same
time, the "Manager" offers something to everyone: "Some people consider Fairs immoral altogether, and eschew such, with
their servants and families: very likely they are right. But persons who think otherwise, and are of a lazy, or a benevolent,
or a sarcastic mood, may perhaps like to step in for half an
hour, and look at the performances. There are scenes of all
sorts: some dreadful combats, some grand and lofty horse-rid-
ing, some scenes of high life, and some of very middling indeed; some love-making for the sentimental, and some light
comic business." [22] In this way the "Manager" tries to entice
different types of visitors to enter his Fair—bearing in mind
the fact that such a visit will also have its aftereffects. After
the reader has been following the narrator for quite some time,
he is informed: "This, dear friends and companions, is my ami-
able object—to walk with you through the Fair, to examine
the shops and shows there; and that we should all come home
after the flare, and the noise, and the gaity, and be perfectly
miserable in private." [23] But the reader will only feel miserable
after walking through the Fair if, unexpectedly, he has come
upon himself in some of the situations, thereby having his attention drawn to his own behavior, which shone out at him
from the mirror of possibilities. The narrator is only pretend-
ing to help the reader—in reality he is goading him.

[20] W. M. Thackeray, *Vanity Fair*, The Centenary Biographical
Edition, ed. Lady Ritchie, I (London, 1910), liii.

[21] *Ibid.*, p. liv.   [22] *Ibid.*   [23] *Ibid.*, p. 225.

His reliability is already reduced by the fact that he is continually donning new masks: at one moment he is an observer of the Fair, like the reader; [24] then he suddenly is blessed with extraordinary knowledge, though he can explain ironically that "novelists have the privilege of knowing everything"; [25] and then, toward the end, he announces that the whole story was not his own at all, but that he overheard it in a conversation.[26] Thus at the beginning of the novel the narrator is presented as the "Manager of the Performance," and at the end he presents himself as the reporter of a story which fell into his hands purely by chance. The further away he stands from the social reality depicted, the clearer becomes the outline of the part he is meant to play. But the reader can only view the social panorama in the constantly shifting perspectives which are opened up for him by this Protean narrator. Although he cannot help following the views and interpretations of the narrator, it is essential for him to understand the motivations behind this constant changing of viewpoints, because only the discovery of the motivations can lead to the comprehension of what is intended. Thus the narrator regulates the distance between reader and events, and in doing so brings about the aesthetic effect of the story. The reader is given only as much information as will keep him oriented and interested, but the narrator deliberately leaves open the inferences that are to be drawn from this information. Consequently empty spaces are bound to occur, spurring the reader's imagination to detect the assumption which might have motivated the narrator's attitude. In this way, we get involved because we react to the viewpoints advanced by the narrator.

[24] See *ibid.*, p. 236, and II, 431.   [25] *Ibid.*, I, 29.

[26] See *ibid.*, II, 344 and 404.

When the "Manager of the Performance" introduces his characters at the beginning of the novel, he says of Becky: "The famous little Becky Puppet has been pronounced to be uncommonly flexible in the joints, and lively on the wire."[27] That the characters are "puppets" is brought home to the reader throughout the novel by the fact that the narrator lets them act on a level of consciousness far below his own. This almost overwhelming superiority of the narrator over his characters—he often depicts them in the light of a knowledge which at best could only have been arrived at by anticipating future events—also puts the reader in a privileged position, though he is never allowed to forget that he should draw his own conclusions from the extra knowledge imparted to him by the narrator. There is even an allegory of the reader's task in the novel, when Becky is basking in the splendor of a grand social evening:

The man who brought her refreshment and stood behind her chair, had talked her character over with the large gentleman in motley-coloured clothes at his side. Bon Dieu! it is awful, that servants' inquisition! You see a woman in a great party in a splendid saloon, surrounded by faithful admirers, distributing sparkling glances, dressed to perfection, curled, rouged, smiling and happy:—Discovery walks respectfully up to her, in the shape of a huge powdered man with large calves and a tray of ices—with Calumny (which is as fatal as truth)— behind him, in the shape of the hulking fellow carrying the wafer-biscuits. Madam, your secret will be talked over by those men at their club at the public-house to-night. . . . Some people ought to have mutes for servants in Vanity Fair— mutes who could not write. If you are guilty, tremble. That fellow behind your chair may be a Janissary with a bow-string

[27] *Ibid.*, I, lv.

in his plush breeches pocket. If you are not guilty, have a care
of appearances: which are as ruinous as guilt.[28]

This little scene contains a change of standpoints typical of
the way in which the reader's observations are conditioned
throughout this novel. The servants are suddenly transformed
into allegorical figures in order to uncover what lies hidden
beneath the façades of their masters. But the discovery will
only turn into calumny from the standpoint of the person af-
fected. The narrator compares the destructive effect of calumny with that of truth, and advises his readers to employ
mutes, or better still illiterate mutes, as servants, in order to
protect themselves against discovery. Then he brings the reader's view even more sharply into focus, finally leaving him to
himself with an indissoluble ambiguity: if the reader feels
guilty because he pretends to be something he is not, then he
must fear those around him as if they were an army of Janis-
saries. If he has nothing to hide, then the social circle merely
demands of him to keep up appearances; but since this is just
as ruinous as deliberate hypocrisy, it follows that life in society
imposes rules on all concerned, reducing human behavior to
the level of play-acting. All the characters in the novel are
caught up in this play, as is expressly shown by the narrator's
own stage metaphor at the beginning and at the end. The key
word for the reader is "discover," and the narrator prods him
along the road to discovery, laying a trail of clues for him to
follow.

The aesthetic effect of *Vanity Fair* depends on activating
the reader's critical faculties so that he may recognize the social reality of the novel as a confusing array of sham attitudes,
and experience the exposure of this sham as the true reality.

[28] *Ibid.*, II, 112.

Instead of being expressly stated, the criteria for such judgments have to be inferred. They are the blanks which the reader is supposed to fill in, thus bringing his own criticism to bear.

A novel can allow for a much fuller expression of this sensed penumbra of unrealized possibilities, of all the what-might-have-beens of our lives. It is because of this that the novel permits a much greater liberty of such speculation on the part of the reader than does the play. . . . The character moves in the full depth of his conditional freedom; he is what he is but he might have been otherwise. Indeed the novel does not merely allow for this liberty of speculation; sometimes it encourages it to the extent that our sense of conditional freedom in this aspect becomes one of the ordering structural principles of the entire work.[29]

The "Manager of the Performance" opens up a whole panorama of views on the reality described, which can be seen from practically every social and human standpoint. The reader is offered a host of different perspectives, and so is almost continually confronted with the problem of how to make them consistent. This is all the more complicated as it is not just a matter' of forming a view of the social world described, but of doing so in face of a rich variety of viewpoints offered by the commentator. There can be no doubt that the author wants to induce his reader to assume a critical attitude toward the social reality portrayed, but at the same time he gives him the alternative of adopting one of the views offered him, or of developing one of his own. This choice is not without a certain amount of risk. If the reader adopts one of the attitudes suggested by the author, he must automatically exclude the oth-

[29] W. J. Harvey, *Character and the Novel* (London, 1965), p. 147.

ers. If this happens, the impression arises, in this particular
novel, that one is looking more at oneself than at the event described. There is an unmistakable narrowness in every standpoint, and in this respect the reflection the reader will see of
himself will be anything but complimentary. But if the reader
then changes his viewpoint, in order to avoid this narrowness,
he will undergo the additional experience of finding that his
behavior is very like that of the two girls who are constantly
adapting themselves in order to rise up the social scale. All the
same, his criticism of the girls appears to be valid. Is it not a
reasonable assumption, then, that the novel was constructed as a
means of turning the reader's criticism of social opportunism
back upon himself? This is not mentioned specifically in the
text, but it happens all the time. Thus, instead of society, the
reader finds himself to be the object of criticism.

Thackeray once mentioned casually: "I have said somewhere
it is the unwritten part of books that would be the most
interesting." [30] It is in the unwritten part of the book that the
reader has his place—hovering between the world of the
characters and the guiding sovereignty of the "Manager of the
Performance." If he comes too close to the characters, he
learns the truth of what the narrator told him at the beginning: "The world is a looking-glass, and gives back to every
man the reflection of his own face." [31] If he stands back with
the narrator to look at things from a distance, he sees through
all the activities of the characters. Through the variableness of
his own position, the reader experiences the meaning of *Vanity
Fair*. As this basic fabric of the novel is not set out in words,
the written text would then be nothing more than the shadow

[30] W. M. Thackeray, *The Letters and Private Papers*, ed. Gordon
N. Ray (London, 1945), III, 391.

[31] Thackeray, *Vanity Fair*, I, 12.

thrown by this unformulated base. This would mean, in turn, that the text is constructed in such a way that it provokes the reader constantly to supplement what he is reading. This act of completion, however, is not concerned merely with secondary aspects of the work, but with the central intention of the text itself. Whenever this occurs, it is clear that the author is not mobilizing his reader because he himself cannot finish off the work he has started; his motive is to bring about an intensified participation which will compel the reader to be that much more aware of the intention of the text.

If the reader of *Vanity Fair* connects the many positions offered him in the text, he will not find the ideal critical stance from which everything will become clear; he will, rather, find himself frequently placed in that very society which he is to criticize.

The reader of the Fielding novel had to coordinate or reconcile respectively two contrary positions and was expected ultimately to find the right balance. The multiplicity of gaps in *Vanity Fair*, however, makes it inevitable that the reader should reveal a great deal of himself if he makes use of the scope of comprehension offered him. Against the background of *Vanity Fair*, the indeterminacy of *Ulysses* seems as if it had gone right out of control. And yet, this novel only attempts to portray a single ordinary day. The subject, then, is considerably reduced when one thinks of the fact that Thackeray wanted to paint a picture of Victorian society, and Fielding one of human nature itself. Clearly, the amount of indeterminacy does not depend on the size of the theme. Moreover, *Ulysses* contains nearly every trick of description and narration that the novel has developed in the course of its relatively short history—and all this for the simple purpose of depicting complete ordinariness? Is it, perhaps, not so much a question of describing everyday reality as conveying the conditions under which it is experienced? [32]

If this is so, then the theme is only the initial impulse, and it is the attempts to deal with the theme that are all-important; for everyday reality does not, in this book, reflect some hidden meaning. In *Ulysses* there are no longer any ideals underlying the world portrayed. Instead, there is an unprecedented wealth of viewpoints and textual patterns which the reader at first finds confusing.

The *Aeolus* chapter is a striking example for the point in question. Bloom's visit to the newspaper office provides the framework for a curiously patterned form of narration. Analysis reveals two separate levels of the text, which one might call, for the sake of convenience, the micro- and the macrostructure of the chapter. The microstructural level consists of a large number of allusions which basically can be divided into three different groups: (1) those dealing with the immediate situation, Bloom's effort to place an advertisement at the newspaper office and the events connected with it; (2) those referring to completely different episodes outside the chapter itself, sometimes relating to incidents already described, and sometimes anticipating things; (3) those passages which seem to slide into obscurity when one tries to work out exactly where they might be heading. However, as these allusions are not distinctly separated but are in fact woven into an intricate pattern, each one of them tends to entice the reader to follow it. Thus the allusions themselves turn into microperspectives which, because of their very density, simply cannot be fol-

---

[32] For details see my forthcoming article, "Der Archetyp als Leerform: Erzählschablonen und Kommunikation in Joyces *Ulysses*," in *Poetik und Hermeneutik*, IV, ed. M. Fuhrmann (Munich, 1971), 369–408.

lowed through to the end. They form abbreviated extracts from reality which inevitably compel the reader to a process of selection.

This is also true of the other stylistic pattern to be discerned within the microstructural stratum. Just as with the allusions, there is throughout an abrupt alternation between dialogue, direct and indirect speech, authorial report, first-person narrative, and interior monologue. Although such techniques do impose a certain order on the abundance of allusions, they also invest them with differing importance. An allusion by the author himself certainly has a function for the context different from one that is made in direct speech by one of the characters. Thus extracts from reality and individual events are not contracted merely into allusions, but, through the different patterns of style, emerge in forms that endow them with a varied range of relevance. At the same time, the unconnected allusions and the abrupt alternation of stylistic devices disclose a large number of empty spaces.

All this gives rise to the stimulating quality of the text. On the one hand, the density of allusions and the continual segmentation of style involve an incessant changing of perspectives, which seem to go out of control whenever the reader tries to pin them down; on the other hand, the empty spaces resulting from cuts and abbreviations tempt the reader to fill them in. He will try to group things, because this is the only way in which he can recognize situations or understand characters in the novel.

The macrostructure of the chapter lends itself to this need for "grouping," though in a peculiar way. Heading and "newspaper column" form the schema that incorporates the allusions and stylistic changes. The heading is an instruction as to what to expect. But the text which follows the caption re-

veals the composition described above, and so in most cases
does not fulfill the expectation raised by the heading. As the
newspaper headlines refer to various incidents in the city of
Dublin, the situation of Ireland, and so forth, they would seem
to be concerned with everyday events, the reality of which is
beyond question. But the column that follows frustrates this
expectation, not only by leading commonplace realities off in
unforeseeable directions, thus destroying the grouping effect of
the headline, but also by fragmenting facts and occurrences in
such a way that to comprehend the commonplace becomes a
real effort. While the heading appears to gratify our basic need
for grouping, this need is predominantly subverted by the text
that follows.

In this chapter, the reader not only learns something about
the events in Dublin on June 16, 1904, but he also experiences
the difficulties inherent in the comprehension of the barest
outline of events. It is precisely because the heading suggests a
way of grouping from a particular viewpoint that the text itself seems so thoroughly to contradict our familiar notions of
perception. The text appears to defy transcription of the circumstances indicated and instead offers the reader nothing but
attitudes or possibilities of perception concerning these circumstances. In exploiting these possibilities, the reader is stimulated to a form of activity that B. Ritchie, in another context,
has described as follows:

The solution to this paradox is to find some ground for distinction between "surprise" and "frustration." Roughly, the
distinction can be made in terms of the effects which the two
kinds of experiences have upon us. Frustration blocks or
checks activity. It necessitates new orientation for our activity,
if we are to escape the cul de sac. Consequently, we abandon
the frustrating object and return to blind impulsive activity.

On the other hand, surprise merely causes a temporary cessation of the exploratory phase of the experience, and a recourse to intense contemplation and scrutiny. In the latter phase the surprising elements are seen in their connection with what has gone before, with the whole drift to the experience, and the enjoyment of these values is then extremely intense. . . . [A]ny aesthetic experience tends to exhibit a continuous interplay between "deductive" and "inductive" operations.[33]

Now it does sometimes occur in this chapter that the expectations aroused by the headings are fulfilled. At such moments, the text seems banal,[34] for when the reader has adjusted himself to the nonfulfillment of his expectations, he will view things differently when they *are* fulfilled. The reason for this is easy to grasp. If the text of the column does not connect up with the heading, the reader must supply the missing links. His participation in the intention of the text is thus enhanced. If the text does fulfill the expectations aroused by the heading, no removing of gaps is required of the reader and he feels the "letdown" of banality. In this way, the textual pattern in this chapter arouses continual conflicts with the reader's own modes of perception, and as the author has completely withdrawn from this montage of possibilities, the reader is given no guidance as to how to resolve the conflicts. But it is through these very conflicts, and the confrontation with the array of different possibilities, that the reader of such a text is given the impression that something does happen to him.

The innumerable facets of this everyday reality have the effect of seeming as if they were merely suggested to the reader

[33] B. Ritchie, "The Formal Structure of the Aesthetic Object," in *The Problems of Aesthetics*, ed. E. Vivas and M. Krieger (New York, 1965), pp. 230 f.

[34] See James Joyce, *Ulysses* (London, 1937), p. 118.

for observation. The various perspectives as provided by the other chapters of the novel abruptly join up, overlap, are segmented, even clash, and through their very density they begin to overtax the reader's vision. The density of the presentational screen, the confusing montage and its interplay of perspectives, the invitation to the reader to look at identical incidents from many conflicting points of view—all this makes it extremely difficult for the reader to find his way. The novel refuses to divulge any principle of how to bind together this interplay of perspectives, and so the reader is forced to provide his own liaison. This has the inevitable consequence that reading becomes a process of selection, with the reader's own imagination providing the criteria for the selection. For the text of *Ulysses* only offers the conditions that make it possible to conceive of this everyday world—conditions which each reader will exploit in his own way. Whenever this happens, "consistent reading suggests itself and illusion takes over." [35]

Yet it is difficult to sustain this illusion in the reading process, for all the eighteen chapters of the novel are written in continually changing styles, so that the view conveyed by each particular style can only be regarded as a suggestion for observation. What, then, does the achievement of the various modes of presentation consist of? First, one can say that they bring to bear a form of observation which underlies the very structure of perception. For we "have the experience of a world, not understood as a system of relations which wholly determine each event, but as an open totality the synthesis of which is inexhaustible. . . . From the moment that experience

[35] Gombrich, *Art and Illusion*, p. 278. Although this quotation is related to a discussion of Constable, it nonetheless presents a point of view which is central in the thesis developed by Gombrich, a thesis whose validity is not limited to painting.

—that is, the opening on to our de facto world—is recognized as the beginning of knowledge, there is no longer any way of distinguishing a level of a priori truths and one of factual ones, what the world must necessarily be and what it actually is." [36] Through their countless offshoots, the different styles of *Ulysses* preclude any meaning directed toward integration, but they also fall into a pattern of observation that contains within itself the possibility of a continual extension. It is the very abundance of perspectives that conveys the abundance of the world under observation.

The effect of this continual change is dynamic, unbounded as it proves to be by any recognizable teleology. From one chapter to the next the "horizon" of everyday life is altered and constantly shifted from one area to another through the links which the reader tries to establish between the chapter styles. Each chapter prepares the "horizon" for the next, and it is the process of reading that provides the continual overlapping and interweaving of the views presented by each of the chapters. The reader is stimulated into filling the "empty spaces" between the chapters in order to group them into a coherent whole. This process, however, has the following results: the conceptions of everyday life which the reader forms undergo constant modifications in the reading process. Each chapter provides a certain amount of expectation concerning the next chapter. The gaps of indeterminacy which open up between the chapters, however, tend to diminish the importance of these expectations as a means of orienting the reader. As the process continues, a "feedback" effect is bound to develop, arising from the new chapter and reacting upon the preceding, which under this new and somewhat unexpected

[36] M. Merleau-Ponty, *Phenomenology of Perception*, trans. Colin Smith (New York, 1962), pp. 219 and 221.

impression is subjected to modifications in the reader's mind. The more frequently the reader experiences this effect, the more cautious and the more differentiated will be his expectations as they arise through his realization of the text. Thus what has just been read modifies what had been read before, so that the reader himself operates the "fusion of the horizons," with the result that he produces an experience of reality which is real insofar as it happens. Reality, then, is a process of realization necessitating the reader's involvement, because only the reader can bring it about. This is why the chapters are not arranged in any sequence of situations that might be complementary to one another; in fact, the unforeseen difference of style rather seems to make each chapter into a turning point as opposed to a continuation. And as the whole novel consists of such turning points, the connections between the chapters appear as indeterminate gaps which in turn do not permit of any clear-cut link, so that the process of reading unfolds itself as a continual modification of all previous conceptions.

The novel opposes the desire for consistency which we constantly reveal when we are reading. Here we are confronted with a gamut of possible reactions. We may be annoyed by all these gaps, which arise in fact through the overprecision of presentation, but this would be like a confession on our part, for it would mean that we prefer to be pinned down by texts, forgoing our own judgment. In this case, we obviously expect literature to present us with a world that has been cleared of contradictions.[37] If we try to break down the areas of indeterminacy in the text, the picture that we draw for ourselves will then be, to a large extent, illusory, precisely because it is so determinate. The illusion arises from a desire for harmony, and it is solely the product of the reader.

[37] See Reinhard Baumgart, *Aussichten des Roman oder Hat Litera tur Zunkunft?* (Neuwied and Berlin, 1968), p. 79.

This marks an important development. The realistic novel of the nineteenth century set out to give its reader an illusion of reality; in *Ulysses*, the high degree of indeterminacy has the effect of rendering illusory any meaning ascribed to everyday reality. The indeterminacy of the text sends the reader off on a search for meaning. In order to find it, he has to mobilize all the forces of his imagination. And in doing this, he has the chance of becoming a discriminating reader, in that he realizes his projected meanings can never fully cover the possibilities of the text. By exposing the limitations inherent in any meaning, modern literature offers the discriminating reader a chance to come to grips with his own ideas.

In some modern texts, this fact can be studied under almost experimental conditions. The works of Beckett are among those whose indeterminacy content is so high that they are often equated with a massive allegorization. The tendency to regard them as allegories is in itself a kind of exasperated form of meaning projection. What causes this exasperation, which can clearly only be pacified by imposing some meaning on the text? Beckett's works, with their extreme indeterminacy, cause a total mobilization of the reader's imagination; the effect of this, however, is that the totally mobilized world of imagination finds itself to be powerless when called upon to explain. And yet this impotence on the part of one's own imagination seems to be necessary if one is to accept Beckett's work at all, for the individuality of his texts only becomes apparent when the world of our imagination is left behind. It is not surprising, therefore, that one's first reaction is to mount a massive operation of meaning projection in order to haul the texts back within the limits of normal thinking.

If fiction stubbornly refuses to reveal the sought-for meaning, then the reader will decide what it has to mean. But then one realizes that by imposing an allegorical or unequivocal

meaning onto the texts, one's approach tends to be superficial
or even trivial. Should not this allegorization be seen as an indication of the nature of our current conceptions and preconceptions rather than as a means of explaining the text? If so,
then such texts will show us the fundamental lack of freedom
resulting from our self-imposed confinement within the world
of our own ideas. In making his reader experience the embar-
rassing predicament of the failure of his understanding, Beckett
opens up a road to freedom which can be embarked on whenever we are prepared to shed our preconceived notions that so
far have dominated our outlook.

The works of Beckett provoke a desire for understanding
which can only be satisfied if we apply our own ideas to the
text, to have them duly rejected as redundant. It is precisely
this process which both stimulates and exasperates us, for who
likes to learn that his own ideas have to be subjected to a fundamental revision if they are to grasp phenomena which seem
to lie beyond their scope? [38]

V

At this point, we are on the verge of leaving our historical
perspective of indeterminacy, which so far has revealed that an
increase in degree resulted in a proportionally enhanced involvement of the reader, which in turn could range from
bringing out the author's own premeditated yet unformulated
intention of the text to a gradual entanglement of the reader
with himself, whenever the repair of indeterminacy gives rise
to the generation of meaning. Let us therefore, by way of concluding, examine the consequences of the facts we have out-

[38] For a more detailed discussion see my forthcoming essay,
"When Is the End Not the End? The Idea of Fiction in Beckett."

lined. First of all, we can say that the indeterminate elements of literary prose—perhaps even of all literature—represents the most important link between text and reader. It is the switch that activates the reader in using his own ideas in order to fulfill the intention of the text. This means that it is the basis of a textural structure in which the reader's part is already incorporated.

In this respect, literary texts differ from those which formulate a concrete meaning or truth. Texts of the latter kind are, by their very nature, independent of the individual reader, for the meaning or truth which they express exists independently of any reader's participation. But when the most vital element of a textual structure is the process of reading, it is forced to rely on the individual reader for the realization of a possible meaning or truth. The meaning is conditioned by the text itself, but only in a form that allows the reader himself to bring it out.

An important sentence in semiotics runs: within a system, the lack of one element is important in itself. If one applies this to literature, one will observe that the literary text is characterized by the fact that it does not state its intention, and therefore the most important of its elements is missing. If this is so, then where is one to find the intention of a text? The answer is: in the reader's imagination. While the literary text has its reality not in the world of objects but in the imagination of its reader, it wins a certain precedence over texts which want to make a statement concerning meaning or truth; in short, over those which claim or have an apophantic character. Meanings and truths are, by nature, influenced by their historical position and cannot in principle be set apart from history. The same applies to literature, too, but since the reality of a literary text lies within the reader's imagination, it must, again

by nature, have a far greater chance of transcending its historical position. From this arises the suspicion that literary texts
are resistant to the course of time, not because they represent
eternal values that are supposedly independent of time, but because their structure continually allows the reader to place
himself within the world of fiction.

What is it that makes the reader want to share in the adventures of literature? This question is perhaps more for the an-
thropologist than for the literary critic, but the fact is clear
that people have always tended to enjoy taking part in the fic-
titious dangers of the literary world; they like to leave their
own security and enter into realms of thought and behavior
which are by no means always elevating. Literature simulates
life, not in order to portray it, but in order to allow the reader
to share in it. He can step out of his own world and get into
another, where he can experience extremes of pleasure and
pain without being involved in any consequences whatsoever.
It is this lack of consequence that enables him to experience
things that would be otherwise inaccessible owing to the press-
ing demands of everyday reality. And precisely because the literary text makes no objectively real demand on its readers, it
opens up a freedom that every one can interpret in his own
way. Thus, with every text we learn not only about what we
are reading but also about ourselves, and this process is all the
more effective if what we are supposed to experience is not explicitly stated but has to be inferred. A piece of literature
wishing to exercise an impact and laying claim to some value
has to comply with the basic requirement which Sir Philip
Sidney tersely summed up in his *Defence of Poesie* by saying:
". . . the Poet . . . never affirmeth." [39] It is largely because of

[39] Sir Philip Sidney, *The Defence of Poesie, The Prose Works*, III,
ed. Albert Feuillerat (Cambridge, 1962), 29.

this fact that literary texts are so constructed as to confirm none of the meanings we ascribe to them, although by means of their structure they continually lead us to such projections of meaning. Thus it is perhaps one of the chief values of literature that by its very indeterminacy it is able to transcend the restrictions of time and written word and to give to people of all ages and backgrounds the chance to enter other worlds and so enrich their own lives.

 Edward W. Said

MOLESTATION AND AUTHORITY
IN NARRATIVE FICTION

In its fully developed form as the novel, narrative prose fiction is by no means a type of literature common to all traditions. This, I think, is an important fact. It may not tell us what the novel is, but it can help us to understand what needs the novel fills and what results the novel can be said to have amongst readers, societies, or traditions in which the genre is significant and native. Let me limit myself to a brief example that illustrates some of what I mean. Modern Arabic literature has novels in it, but they are almost entirely of this century. There is no tradition out of which these modern works developed; by and large, they can be accounted for by saying that at some point writers became aware of European novels and began to write works like them in Arabic. Obviously it could not have been just that simple, but it is true that the desire to create a rival alternative world, or to increase, add to, or augment our world in writing (which desire belongs with others at the basis of the novelistic tradition in the West), is inimical to the Islamic world-view. That view sees the world as a plenum, capable neither of diminishment nor of addition. Consequently stories, like those in *The Arabian Nights*, are ornamental, variations on the world, and not completions of it; neither are they lessons, structures, extensions, or totalities designed to illustrate the author's prowess in representation, the education of a character, or ways in which the world can be viewed and changed.

If this is kept in mind then it becomes apparent that one of the most urgent uses of the novel is that it enables the writer to represent characters and societies in development. These characters and societies grow and move because in the novel they are imitations of the process of engenderment and growth possible for the mind to imagine. Therefore novels are aesthetic objects that fill gaps in an incomplete world, they satisfy a human urge to add to reality, and they portray fictional characters in which one can believe. Novels are much more than that, of course. Nevertheless, in this essay I should like to consider the institution of narrative prose fiction as a kind of appetite for wanting personally to modify reality, for wanting to do that by permitting a writer to author a new fictional entity, and for wanting at the same time to accept the consequences of that desire.

In my title I had hoped to indicate the kind of perspective I wish to adopt. Authority to me suggests a series of interesting connections, a constellation of linked meanings. For not only does it mean, as the OED tells us, a power to enforce obedience, or a derived or delegated power, or a power to influence action, or a power to inspire belief, or a person whose opinion is accepted: not only those, but a connection as well with *author*, that is, a person who originates or gives existence to something, a begetter, father, or ancestor, a person also who sets forth written statements. There is still another cluster of meanings. Author is tied to the past participle *auctus*, from the verb *augere*: therefore *auctor*, according to Eric Partridge, is literally an increaser and a founder. *Auctoritas* is production, invention, cause, in addition to meaning a right of possession. Finally, it means continuance, a causing to continue. Taken together these meanings are all grounded in the following notions. First, the power of an individual to initiate, institute, establish. Second, that this power and its product are an increase over what had been there previously. Third, that by its wielding the power possesses its issue and what is derived therefrom. And fourth, that authority maintains the continuity of its course. All four of these abstractions can be used to describe the way in which narrative fiction asserts itself psychologically and aesthetically through the technical efforts of the novelist. Thus—by written statement—inauguration, augmentation by extension, possession, continuity, for the word "authority" in my title.

Now "molestation" is a word I use to describe the bother and responsibility of all these powers and efforts. By that I mean that no novelist is ever unaware that his authority, regardless of how complete, or the authority of a narrator, is a sham. Molestation, then, is a consciousness of one's duplicity, whether one is a character or a novelist. And molestation occurs when novelists and critics have reminded themselves traditionally of how the novel is always subject to a comparison with reality and thereby found to be illusion. Or again, molestation is central to a character's experience of disillusionment during the course of a novel. To speak of authority in narrative prose fiction is also inevitably to be speaking of the molestations that accompany it.

Authority and its molestations are at the root of the fictional process: at least this is the enabling relationship most fiction itself renders. Later we shall examine some reasons for this. But the problematic of fiction is how narrative sets alongside the world of common discourse another discourse whose origin is important, indeed crucial, to it, located as it is in the responsibility taken for it by the begetting speaker. Yet this fictional progenitor is bound by the fact that he is always at a remove from a truly fundamental role. It is no accident, I think, that James and Conrad, those exceptionally reflective craftsmen of fiction, made this distance from a radical origin the theme of much of their best work. *Heart of Darkness* explores origins paradoxically through a series of obscuring narrative frames; borne from one narrative level to another, Marlow's African adventure gains its power from the uniqueness, the strangeness of its persistence in those levels, not unequivocally from the strangeness of the experience itself. The heart of the matter —Kurtz's experience—is posited outside Marlow's discourse, which leaves us to investigate, if we can, the speaker's authority. By the end of the tale we are aware of something given birth to by Marlow that eludes empirical tests, even as it rests most securely upon the fact of its delivery by Marlow. Here in most of its senses authority is involved, except that we are required to accept that authority as never a final one. There is derivation, begetting, continuity, augmentation— and also a nagging, molesting awareness that beyond those there is something still more authentic, to which fiction is secondary.

No writer to my knowledge has so subtly investigated some of these notions as Kierkegaard. To read *The Point of View for My Work as an Author* simply as commentary on his work is to rob it of its most useful insights. For there Kierkegaard is probing what is fundamental to all writing (preeminently fiction and personal discourse) in the center of which is the relationship between a focal character whose voice for the reader is authoritative, and the nature of the authorship entailed by such a voice. It is of a kind with the relationship between Isabel Archer, for example, to the movement of whose consciousness the reader attends very carefully, and the type of writing James had to practice to produce her. Behind both James and Isabel is the generative authority that as secular critics we call imaginative, but which Kierkegaard the Christian called "divine governance" (*Styrelse*). The role of such governance is not described until Kierkegaard has already laid out the principles that have distinguished his work. He has been writing two sorts of book, he says, aesthetic and religious. The former sort seems to contradict the more obviously urgent religious works, but Kierkegaard wants it understood that the aesthetic books were designed, in manner at least, to deal with serious questions in a mode suitable for the frivolity of his contemporaries. Taken alone, then, the aesthetic works would be confusing, not to say hopelessly unserious. But taken as necessary preparations for the directly religious works, his aesthetic writings are *indirect*, ironic communications of higher truths.

Here we have the characteristic Kierkegaardian figure of repetition. The aesthetic works are what he calls a dialectical reduplication of the truth. "For as a woman's coyness has a reference to the true lover and yields when he appears, so, too, dialectical reduplication has a reference to true seriousness." There is a strict connection between aesthetic and religious, one that binds them together in bonds of necessity: the religious is a prior, more important truth given in secondary ironic and dissembling forms. The aesthetic works do not occur in a void, even though it appears otherwise, so striking is the freedom of their expression. We must remember, therefore, that "there is a difference between writing on a blank sheet of paper and bringing to light by the application of a caustic fluid a text which is hidden under another text." The aesthetic hides or signals the religious just as Socrates' comic personality concealed the deepest seriousness. We accept the indirect mode, which seems to nullify the truth in order that the truth might emerge more fully later. This, says Kierkegaard, is a teleological suspension practiced so that the truth may become truer.

Kierkegaard's authorship was a deliberately composite one, and the patron of his enterprise is Socrates, to whom he devoted his master's thesis entitled *The Concept of Irony*. What always interested Kierkegaard was the difficulty of speaking directly to an unresponsive audience about matters of which silence was the most suitable expression. The difficulty, however, reflects as much on the author's weakness as it does on his audience's. In an extremely long footnote to a phrase in Chapter III of *The Point of View* he argues that his total authorship was a *superfluity* only because he depended on God and was a weak human being; otherwise his work would have come to grips with the human situation and "would have been interrelated with the instant and the effective in the instant." So in his aesthetic works Kierkegaard was the strong author whose mode concealed the true weakness vis-à-vis God which the religious author was at pains to reveal. The aesthetic was an ironic double, a dialectical reduplication, of a religious truth. The human author augments and is strong, whereas with regard to the divine he is weak, which causes his work to stand apart and appear superfluous to the here and now.

One aspect of authorship, then, is its contingent authority, its ability to initiate or build structures, whose absolute authority is radically nil, but whose contingent authority is a quite satisfactory transitory alternative to the absolute truth. Therefore the difference between Abraham's true authority in *Fear and Trembling* and the narrator's contingent authority is that Abraham is silent, whereas the narrator universalizes in language; the point is that any absolute truth cannot be expressed in words, for only diminished, flawed versions of the truth are available to language. This is as much as to say that fiction alone speaks or is written—truth has no need of words—and that all voices are assumed. The importance of Kierkegaard's formulations is that he was particularly accurate in describing the tactics of his authorship, with its recourse to revealing pseudonyms, and more generally accurate in describing the tactics of writing that committed the author self-consciously to using an assumed voice. This voice sounds certain because it seems to determine its own way and to validate its pronouncements by acceptable and sometimes dramatic means. Thus Kierkegaard, calling himself Johannes de Silentio in order ironically to remind us how far his words are from Abraham's silence and truth, writes the following mock disclaimer in *Fear and Trembling:*

The present writer is nothing of a philosopher; he is, *poetice et eleganter,* an amateur writer who neither writes the System nor *promises* of the System, who neither subscribes to the System nor ascribes anything to it. He writes because for him it is a luxury which becomes the more agreeable and more evident, the fewer there are who buy and read what he writes.

Yet the assumed voice's authority is a usurped one, for behind the voice is the truth, somehow unapprehendable, irreducible to words, and perhaps even unattractive, to which the voice remains subservient in an entirely interesting way. (Parenthetically, it is perhaps worth suggesting that the novel is the aesthetic form of servitude: no other genre so completely renders the meaning of *secondariness*.) Here again Kierkegaard is very subtle. The relation between truth and its artistic version is dialectical, not strictly mimetic. By dialectical, I mean that Kierkegaard allows to the aesthetic the maximum freedom without losing an awareness of the aesthetic's rewording of the religious, or its precarious status. In other words, we are to understand the dialectical connection as making ironic the convincing pretensions of the aesthetic.

Kierkegaard everywhere insists on the individuality of the aesthetic voice. It is neither abstract nor communal. In an important passage in *The Concept of Irony* he discusses the most distinctive feature of the ironic, aesthetic voice:

But the outstanding feature of irony . . . is the subjective freedom which at every moment has within its power the possibility of a beginning and is not generated from previous conditions. There is something seductive about every beginning because the subject is still free, and this is the satisfaction the ironist longs for. At such moments actuality loses its validity for him; he is free and above it.

What the ironic voice goes on to create is a "usurped totality," of course, based on a seductive beginning. Insofar as an author begins to write at all he is ironic, since for him too there is a deceptive and subjective freedom at the outset. The distance that separates him from actuality is a function of his personality which, Kierkegaard says, "is at least momentarily incommensurable with actuality," and of his continuing, augmenting authority. But we must never forget the abiding truth, from which he departs in search of his new fulfillment.

Kierkegaard's analysis of authorship exposes the uneasiness and vacillations out of which narrative fiction develops. If we suspend for a moment our lifelong familiarity with fiction, and if we try not to take the presence of novels for granted, we will see that the seminal conception of narrative fiction depends simultaneously upon a number of special conditions. The first special condition is that there must be some strong sense of doubt that the authority of any single voice, or group of voices, is sufficient unto itself. In the community formed between reader, author, and character, each individual desires the accompaniment of another voice. Each hears in the other the seductive beginning of a new life, an alternative to his own, and yet each grows progressively aware of an authenticity being systematically betrayed during the course of the partnership—the character most of all. Our interest in Dorothea Brooke is that she has expectations of some life different from the one she presently leads; impelled by those expectations she becomes another person in her marriage to Dr. Casaubon. What she leaves behind during that unhappy episode she later recovers in a form tempered by the experience of self-deception. Dissatisfied with herself at first, she doubles her life by adding a new one to it: she does this by the authority of her personality, yet her travails are no less the result of that molesting authority. So too for Eliot, who creates Dorothea in the enactment of her will to be another. Also the reader, who allows Dorothea the benefit of his doubt about his isolated self.

The inaugural act of usurpation once performed—because of pleasure taken in a free beginning, because of a desire to reduplicate life in a more accessible form—there follows consolidation of the initial gain by various means. One is the accumulation of prerogatives. Notice how skillfully this is done by

Huck Finn at the opening of his narrative, as he asserts his right to tell us *his* version of things:

You don't know about me without you have read a book by the name of *The Adventures of Tom Sawyer*, but that ain't no matter. That book was made by Mr. Mark Twain and he told the truth, mainly. There was things which he stretched, but mainly he told the truth. That is nothing. I never seen anybody but lied one time or another.

Other means are a strengthening belief in one's project, a cultivation of psychological arrangements, and the fixing of useful as well as frightening things in places that are convenient.

Marx has a chapter in *Capital* on "The Secret of Primitive Accumulation" in which he traces the growth of capitalistic society (based on private ownership) from the dissolution of feudal society. His terms need recalling here, since he claims that once the individual has "escaped from the regime of the guilds, their rules for apprenticeship and journeymen, and the impediments of their labour regulations" he becomes a freeseller of himself, and thereby an immediate producer. Of course, Marx comments, this is really an enslavement, for man has been robbed of all his own means of production: he therefore creates others, alternative to his own, and then falls prey to the illusion that he has free labor-power. The real power is elsewhere, but the illusion persists as the individual generates values and prerogatives suitable to his condition. This is perfectly consonant with what Pip does in *Great Expectations*. Self-created, he labors to be a free gentleman with a fancy life while in fact he is enslaved by an outcast who has himself been victimized by society. Pip's schemes grant him the right to manners, thoughts, and actions that dispose of life with grand ease. And it is with the exposure of the falseness of those schemes, as well as with the actual successes he manages, that the novel is concerned.

The systematic reinforcement of illusions, which Marx and Engels had treated earlier in *The German Ideology*, underlies Pip's course in *Great Expectations*. His progress up the social scale is supported by every character in the novel, so committed in thought at least is everyone (Joe Gargery included) to an ideology that equates money with higher privilege, morality, and worth. Although the novel itself licenses Pip's expectations, it also mercilessly undercuts them, mainly by showing that the limit on these expectations is inherent in them. That is, Pip can neither have nor hold expectations without a patron who makes them possible. So Pip's freedom is dependent upon an unnamed patron who requires visits to Jaggers, who requires that no questions be asked, and so on. The more Pip believes he is acting on his own, the more he is drawn into a tightly woven web of circumstances that weighs him down completely; the plot's revelation of accidents that link the principal characters together is Dickens's method of countering Pip's ideology of free upward progress. For Marx, the equivalent of Dickens's plot was history, by which it could be known how one or another "freedom" is a function of class interest and alliances, not really freedom at all: hence the illusion of free labor-power that allows the worker to think he can do as he pleases, whereas in fact he dangles on strings pulled by others.

A second special condition is that the truth—whatever that may be—can only be approached indirectly, by means of a mediation that because of its falseness paradoxically makes the truth truer. In this context a truer truth is one arrived at by a process of elimination: alternatives similar to the truth are shed one by one. The elevation of truth-resembling fictions to preeminence becomes a habitual practice, because fiction is thought to be the trial of truth by error. In trying to account for this rationale we enter a realm of speculation to which the best guide, I think, is Vico. In *The New Science* Vico situates his inquiries at a point of original juncture where three primacies intersect: human identity, human history, and human language. These are also the components with which the novel must work, and which it individualizes. So the correspondence between Vico and the generation of a novel is worth examining. Let us keep in mind first of all that in the center of a novel is the character who, unlike his counterpart in the classical drama, is not conceded to be at the very outset *like* a known figure. Ahab, Julien Sorel, Frederic Moreau, Stavrogin —all these are figures deliberately original; they are not Oedipus, or Agamemnon, in whose portrayal the dramatist relies upon a common mythic past, or upon a community of socially funded values and symbols. A novel's protagonist may resemble a known character, but he is not alleged to *be* that character. Whatever we recognize in the novelistic character we do at another level of much less prominence, that is, at the level of private authority. What is is that antedates private authority will be discussed later.

Authority, says Vico, comes from *auctor*, which "certainly comes from *autos* (proprius or suus ipsius)"; the word's original meaning is property. Property is dependent upon human will and choice; therefore it was axiomatic for Vico that "philology observes the authority of human choice, whence comes consciousness of the certain." So the study of language recovers the conscious choices made by which man created himself and established his authority. Language preserves the traces of these choices, which a philologist can then decipher.

Opposed to philology is philosophy, "which contemplates reason, whence comes knowledge of the true." Note the demarcation: on the one hand, language, authority, and certain identity, on the other hand, the true. Certainty pertains to poetic creation (and its understanding to philology), for creation does its work in three forms of authority, divine, human, and natural. By this Vico means that human history was made by man in three stages of mythologized power, three phases of locating human interests and inventing agencies to maintain them. In the divine phase, the gods fix the giants by chaining them to earth (*terrore defixi*): whatever man fears he divides into a subduing and a subdued power. Thus Jove and the chained giants. In the second or human phase, the giants, who have been wandering the earth, learn to control their bodies, thereby exercising their will. They inhabit caves, and settle there, domesticated. Finally, after a long period of settlement they become lords of dominion, occupation, and possession. A division occurs: the *gentes majores*, or the founders and originators of families, and the people, over whom they rule.

Vico calls this succession of periods poetic history in order to designate not so much a "real" sequence as a retrospective construction. What the construction describes, however, is real enough, even if its figures are highly metaphoric. It is the institution of a humanized abode, populated with beings and maintained by an authority that conserves itself while slowly being reduced from grandiose powers to more and more sharply differentiated functions. The axial moment from which this sequence departs is the Flood, or a great rupture, an event that separates man's history into two distinct types that thereafter flow concurrently with each other: sacred history and gentile history. Of the first Vico has little to say, except that it is in a sort of permanent rapport with God. The second is ours, an alternative to the first. Like Kierkegaard, Vico sees things in a double perspective, aesthetic and religious. And like Kierkegaard he is more at home in the former than in the latter. The important point is that both men see that the aesthetic (or poetic) requires a reconstructive *technique*, gives rise to a special manner of being and to a totality of distinctions, and always has the consciousness of its alternative status. What is most interesting about this alternative consciousness is that it is a valid and even necessary institution of life despite the relative subservience of its position, which we may call aesthetic and ironic with Kierkegaard, or poetic and fictional with Vico.

A third special condition for the generation of fictional narrative is an extraordinary fear of the void that antedates private authority. This, I think, is one of the less noted themes of narrative at least as far back as *Robinson Crusoe*. For in the shipwreck that throws him upon his island wilderness, Crusoe is born—with extinction always threatening afterwards, and with his gained and constantly experienced authority over his domain as the safeguard of his continuing existence. A whole range of principal characters in fiction is premised on the same basis: orphans, outcasts, parvenus, emanations, solitaries, and deranged types whose background is either rejected, mysterious, or unknown. Sterne's fascination with Tristram's birth toys with the seemingly limitless hovering between nullity and existence that is central to the novelistic conception of character, and to its representation in language. Were it not for a rejection of the anonymous void, Ishmael, Pip, Marcel, for example, would be unthinkable. Ishmael pointedly tells us that his narrative of shipboard is a substitute for the philosophical flourish with which Cato threw himself upon his sword. And the bond between the character's novelistic life and the death from which he is stayed while he lasts before us is querulously summed up by James Wait in *The Nigger of the Narcissus* when he announces that "I must live till I die."

In using Marx, Kierkegaard, and Vico to point up requisite conditions for fiction I have tried to parallel their thought with the novel's ground in human experience. As such the philosopher or historian belongs in his work to a common mode of conceiving experience of which another version is the novel. Here we may remark the similarities between thought that produces philosophical works, for instance, and thought that produces novels. Yet the difference is no less crucial. It is a difference in degree. The difference between Kierkegaard's anthropology of authority and, say, Pip's in *Great Expectations* is that Pip is more of an augmenter, continuor, and originator, both because Dickens willed it so and because that is his (Pip's) essence as a character. As to the impulse that has such staying power, and that is not commonly diverted into either philosophy or history (Tolstoy is an exception), we can look to Freud briefly for an explanation.

In any of the reconstructive techniques, be they history, philosophy, or personal narrative, according to Freud the objective is both to create alternatives to a confusing reality and to minimize the pain of experience. In other words, the project is an economic one. Yet insofar as it is also a repetitive procedure it has to do with instincts driving the mind over ground already traveled. Some instincts are life-promoting, others return one to the primal unity of death. The novelistic character gains his fictional authority, as we saw, in the desire to escape death; therefore the narrative process endures so long as that will persists. Yet because a character's real origin is the anonymity of pure negation—and this is nowhere more beautifully described than in the first and last volumes of Proust's novel—there is a simultaneous pressure upon him of what he is always resisting. The demystification, or education, of illusions, which is the novel's central theme, then enacts his increasing molestation by a truer process pushing him to an ending that resembles his beginning out of negation. The sheer length of the classic novel can almost be accounted for by the desire to initiate and promote a reduplication of life and, at the same time, to allow for a convincing portrayal of how that sort of life leads inevitably to the revelation of a merely borrowed authority. The element that contains as well as symbolizes the whole enterprise is, as recent critics have shown, the language of temporal duration.

But whether we depict the narrative in temporal or in verbal terms, the important thing is that one must understand narrative as wholly qualified by the extremely complex authority of its presentation. Pip, Dorothea, and Isabel are flawed by their illusions, by a skewing of their vision of themselves and of others. Yet all three of them *move;* out of them rises a sense of motion and of change that engages our serious interest. For Pip's illusions there are, as an unforgettable counterpoise, Miss Havisham's solitary paralyses: whereas he generates a life for himself whose falseness is more and more manifest, she does next to nothing, memorialized in the sarcophagus of Satis house. Late in the novel he tells her accusingly, "You let me go on": what is enough for her is only the beginning for Pip. And Dorothea's affections and aspirations contrast sharply with Dr. Casaubon's frigid personality, symbolized by his unfinished, locked-up manuscript. Lastly, James contrasts Isabel's flights with Osmond's perfect retreat at Roccanera, the one a beautiful projector, the other a prison from which all humanity has been excluded. Within a novel, then, the principle of authority provides a motion attempting always to steer clear of obstacles that emerge to inhibit, maim, or destroy it utterly. In historical novels of the early nineteenth century there are figures of authority to whom the protagonists are subordinate. Cardinal Borromeo in *I Promesi Sposi* and the King in *Quentin Durward*, to mention only two examples, serve within each novel as reminders of the limits upon a character's secular power; these limits are vestiges of the "real" historical world, the truer realm, remaining in the fiction. Yet their functions will become incorporated into the character's increasing self-consciousness of his weakness in the world, in the way the Marshalsea Prison in *Little Dorrit* is still more a psychological molestation of poor Mr. Dorrit when he is free than even it was in reality.

Those are outer circumstances, however, that exist at the level of plot. I want to return now to the level of authoritative character as the novel's conceiving matrix. Sometimes, as in Goethe's *Die Wahlverwandschaften* or in Laclos's *Les Liaisons dangereuses*, the fiction is sustained by pairs whose destiny is always a coupled one. Edward, Ottilie, and Charlotte produce Goethe's story through a complex series of partnerships whose permanence is practically ontological to the novel's existence; similarly Valmont and Merteuil, whose schemes together are the veritable abstract without which the plot could not be. Richardson's Clarissa, in comparison, is an example of private authority resisting interventions, and yet beseeching Lovelace's interventions by the deep attractiveness of her inviolate privacy. In the case of Pip—which I want to analyze a little now—we have a remarkably economical individual character. From Pip, Dickens is able to derive a very diverse range of originating circumstances (circumstances that give rise to an entire world), which taken as a group can serve as a perfect example of the authoritative or authorizing fictional consciousness. The more remarkable is this economy when we realize that Dickens makes use of every traditional narrative device —development, climax, linear plot sequence, physical setting, realistic accuracy of detail—together with a thoroughly imagined method of using them, in so complete a way that even James and Eliot cannot match him, I think. *Great Expectations* reposes upon Dickens's portrayal of Pip as together the novel's condition for being, or the novel's action, and for character in it: this gives the notions of authority and molestation I have been discussing an archetypal form. The first-person narration adds to the purity of Dickens's achievement.

Pip's name, we are immediately told by him, is what he can just cope with by mixing remnants no longer meaningful to him but inherited by him (Philip Pirrip) "on the authority" of his parents' tombstone and by his sister's command. He lives, then, as an alternative being: as an orphan without real parents, and as a harassed surrogate son to a much older sister. All through the novel the initial division will be perpetuated. On the one hand there is the natural, true genealogy that is banished from the novel at the outset, but which makes its appearance fitfully through Joe, Biddy, and the new little Pip who springs up near the novel's end. The fact that Joe Gargery is like a father to him, though in fact his brother-in-law, makes Pip's alienation from the family continuity more poignant. For the other great division in the novel's order is a substitute family, which has its roots in the unpleasant household of Mrs. Joe. Once established by Dickens, this order recurs throughout, with Pip going from one to another incarnation of it. This is the novel's most insistent pattern of narrative organization: how Pip situates himself at the center of several family groups, families whose authority he challenges by trying to institute his own through great expectations, but which finally destroy him. Each family is revealed successively to belong in the sphere of another more dominant, and prior, one. Miss Havisham's and Estella's circle later admits Jaggers, then Magwitch, then Molly and Compeyson. And after each revelation Pip finds himself a little more self-implicated and a little less central.

In this other division Dickens allows Pip to see how, even though he seems occasionally to be fortunate, there is a necessary connection between himself and prison and crime. Those fearful things are real enough, as are, too, the harshness of his childhood, the schemes of Magwitch and Miss Havisham (his alternate parents), and the bankruptcy to which he arrives later on. Set against this theme is the motif of reassembling unpleasant fragments—for nothing is given whole to Pip, or to anyone else—into new, fabricated units. A little sojourn at Miss Havisham's is made up by Pip into an extraordinary adventure which, despite Joe's solemn warnings, he will repeat again and again. The ironical significance of Pip's constructions is accentuated by Wemmick's house, that fantastic melange of remnants wrenched into a mock-medieval castle by the man's irrepressible desire to create a better life at Falworth; and also by Wopsle's acting, for which Shakespeare is only a beginning excuse for a rather free improvisation. These, like Pip, are *bricoleurs*, who "brought up by hand," by fits and starts, assert their authority over the threats of unpleasant dispersion. The image of a fabricating hand and its cognates is carried over into almost every corner of the novel: chains are filed, a release, hands retied differently. Pip is linked by strong hands with Magwitch's compensatory impulses, with Miss Havisham's, and, through Estella, with Molly's exceptionally powerful hands. After his breakdown, Pip finds himself reposing like a baby in Joe's paternal arms.

The basic scheme I have been describing is the cycle of

birth and death. Pip's origin as a novelistic character is rooted
in the death of his parents. By his wish to make up for that
long series of graves and tombstones he creates a way for himself, and yet with the novel's duration, one route after another
is blocked, and dies, only to have him force another. Like Isabel and Dorothea, Pip as a character is conceived as excess,
wanting more, trying to be more than in fact he is. The aug-
mentations are finally all based in the death from which he
springs, and to which he returns at the end. Only by then a
new, more authentic dispensation has been bred, and which finally yields up a new little Pip. Between them the two Pips
cover the spread whose double axis is true life on the one
hand, and novelistic life on the other. Both Dickens and Flaubert in *Madame Bovary* use money to signify the protagonists'
transitory power to shore up their authority to dream and
even for a while to be something they cannot remain for long.
Catherine, the aged farm-worker, little Pip, Joe, and Biddy—
these are the inarticulate, abiding natures that money cannot
touch nor illusion tempt.

Together little Pip and old Pip are Dickens's way of aligning
the molestations of truth against an imperious authority badly
in need of checks. That Dickens does so explicitly only near
the novel's end is a sign of how, late in his novelistic career, he
had come to see the problem of authority as rooted in the self
and therefore primarily checked by the self: hence little Pip
appears only to *confirm* Pip's transgression, his subsequent education, and his irremediable alienation from the family of
man. One way of noting Dickens's acute understanding of the
self's way with itself is that in *Great Expectations* Pip under-
goes experiences of mystification and demystification on his
own, within himself; whereas in *Martin Chuzzlewit*, two es-

tranged Martins, one young and one old, educate each other into a family embrace. In the later novel Dickens represented the harsher principles of authority—that at bottom the self wants its own way, unshared by anyone else, and that its awakening to truth entails a still more unpleasant alienation from others—which in the earlier one he had divided between a pair of misunderstanding, willful relatives. The self's authority splits apart again later in the century, in, for example, *The Picture of Dorian Gray*, *The Strange Case of Dr. Jekyll and Mr. Hyde*, and, later still, in "The Secret Sharer." In all three works, however, the alter-ego is a hidden reminder of the primary self's unstable authority. Jekyll's sense of "the fortress of identity" includes as well a recognition that the fortress has hideous, molesting foundations. Dickens refused to embody these recognitions *outside* the individual as Wilde, Stevenson, and Conrad would. Doubtless he saw Pip's predicament as one communally shared and even abetted. But nowhere is there any excuse for Pip, neither orphanhood, poverty, nor circumstance, that reduces the deliberateness of his choices, his individual responsibility, and his often venal compromises with reality, all of which return finally to burden him:

That I had a fever and was avoided, that I suffered greatly, that I often lost my reason, that the time seemed interminable, that I confounded impossible existences with my own identity; that I was a brick in the house wall, and yet entreating to be released from the giddy place where the builders had set me; that I was a steel beam of a vast engine, clashing and whirling over a gulf, and yet that I implored in my own person to have the engine stopped, and my part in it hammered off; that I passed through these phases of disease, I know of my own remembrance, and did in some sort know at the time.

After that he can only be "a weak helpless creature" and thankful for the Gargery family's solicitude; he remains an orphan.

Yet Pip's history begins with the loss of a family and—no less important—with a kindness performed out of fear. Pip's act of terrified charity is the germ of his later experience; so far as the plot is concerned, it is the author of his history and, of course, of his troubles. One might be perhaps too rash to say that in its origins at least Pip's act, with its extended consequences, is an aesthetic dialectic reduplication, even an ironic one, of the charity we associate with Christ's ministry and agony. And yet, directly or not, novels too reflect the ethos of the Christian West. The original instance of divine errancy, the Incarnation, transformed God into man, an alternative being: the record of that mystery is given in language that only approximates the deed. So, we might say, novels represent that process and its record at many removes, and after many secular transformations. The attribution of authority to a character by a writer, the implementation of that authority in a narrative form, and the burdens and difficulties submitted to as a result: all these are ways by which the almost numinous communal institutions of language accept and conserve the imprint of an individual force. If in the end these institutions chasten the individual, it is because he needs to be reminded that private authority is part of, but cannot fully be, an integral truth. Fiction's authority repeats that insight, leaving the truth to a higher governance—outside the genre, but like it in possessing a principle of creativity. The real irony is how fiction makes us believe that the analogy holds.

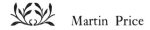 Martin Price

THE IRRELEVANT DETAIL AND
THE EMERGENCE OF FORM

The problem with which to start is the irrelevant detail. Every realistic novel gives us innumerable details: how people look, what they wear, where they live. We generally accept these details as what Henry James called "solidity of specification." [1] They give us the air of reality, the illusion of life, without which the novel can hardly survive. Elizabeth Bowen puts this another way: "The novel lies, in saying something happened that did not. It must, therefore, contain uncontradictable truth, to warrant the original lie." [2] Yet clearly there can be no end to such specification if we allow it full range. At what point do we set limits and by what means? Can there be pure irrelevance? And, if not, what degrees of irrelevance can we admit?

When we read a novel, we adjust more or less insensibly to

[1] "The Art of Fiction" (1884), reprinted in F. O. Matthiessen, *The James Family* (New York, 1947), p. 360.

[2] "Notes on Writing a Novel," in *Collected Impressions* (London, 1950), p. 249.

the kind of relevance it establishes. We may prepare for an expansive exploration of the setting, for a solid evocation of the
virtual past. Or we may settle instead for a deep descent into a
consciousness, only surmising from rumination and memory
the world that surrounds it. Or we may adapt to an undefined
locale, perhaps one with strange, gamelike rules of probability,
where encounters obey laws we can only puzzle our way into
grasping. The reader is apt to find the right key, to frame appropriate expectations, and to give himself up to the terms of
the fictional contract the author has established. To discover
such canons of relevance may require little effort in a conventional work; it may be a major source of interest in the experimental novel, where the experiment is performed upon the
reader as well as upon the material.

In the realistic novel we expect the principal characters to
have a broad range of attributes, and we assume that the more
attributes they have, the less important some must be. What of
the color of the heroine's hair? In archetypal romance blond
hair all but commands a state of innocence, gentility, and
moral earnestness, whereas dark hair promises commanding
will, adroitness, and a strong instinctive life. That is, the typol-
ogy of romance is such that attributes are comparatively few
and are tightly coordinated. In realistic novels the color of hair
need not imply moral attributes; there is a lower degree of relevance imposed, and some attributes seem to be given only to
create a convincingly full portrait. Yet even there we are in-
clined to seek significance, to expect a higher degree of relevance than the writer seems to claim. This may reflect the tendency we have in our own experience to create patterns, to
relate elements, to simplify, to classify. Our first impressions
are often based upon stereotypes, upon conventional categories
by which we assimilate the unfamiliar or bewildering. It is

only with closer knowledge and extended interest that we begin to differentiate, to specify distinctive patterns or telling peculiarities, to construct an individual.

Let us consider briefly the introduction of Mary and Henry Crawford into Jane Austen's *Mansfield Park*. Mary Crawford has lost her London home and is seeking, with some misgivings, "to hazard herself among her other relations." The first meeting is auspicious:

Miss Crawford found a sister without preciseness or rusticity —a sister's husband who looked a gentleman, and a house commodious and well fitted up; and Mrs. Grant received in those whom she hoped to love better than ever, a young man and woman of very prepossessing appearance. Mary Crawford was remarkably pretty; Henry, though not handsome, had air and countenance; the manners of both were lively and pleasant, and Mrs. Grant immediately gave them credit for everything else.[3]

Mr. Grant, although a parson, looks a gentleman; the Crawfords have a "very prepossessing appearance." The only attributes of Mrs. Grant that are noted are her manners and her facilities for entertainment; and the Crawfords, too, are surveyed for their promise as diverting visitors.

In the next chapter, the Crawfords are studied more closely by Maria and Julia Bertram, the two willful and self-absorbed daughters of Sir Thomas:

Miss Crawford's beauty did her no disservice with the Miss Bertrams. They were too handsome themselves to dislike any woman for being so too, and were almost as much charmed as their brothers, with her lively dark eye, clear brown complexion, and general prettiness. Had she been tall, full formed, and

[3] *Mansfield Park*, Vol. I, Ch. 4.

fair, it might have been more of a trial; but as it was there could be no comparison, and she was most allowably a sweet pretty girl, while they were the finest young women in the country.[4]

We notice that Mary Crawford's "clear brown complexion" is admitted in contrast to the Miss Bertrams' fairness; but it is only one element in the image of a "sweet pretty girl," that self-comforting category under which Maria and Julia can accept her presence. To go on:

Her brother was not handsome; no, when they first saw him, he was absolutely plain, black and plain; but still he was the gentleman, with a very pleasing address. The second meeting proved him not so very plain; he was plain, to be sure, but then he had so much countenance, and his teeth were so good, and he was so well made, that one soon forgot he was plain; and after a third interview, after dining in company with him at the parsonage, he was no longer to be called so by anybody. He was, in fact, the most agreeable young man the sisters had ever known, and they were equally delighted with him. Miss Bertram's engagement made him in equity the property of Julia, of which Julia was fully aware, and before he had been at Mansfield a week, she was quite ready to be fallen in love with.

Jane Austen uses *style indirect libre*, indirect discourse that catches the idiom of a character but may compress his reasoning, as a speeded-up film mechanizes motion. Through it she catches the rapid, almost mechanical process of rationalization by which a marriageable gentleman is found to have extraordinary charms. Henry's somewhat undistinguished appearance is searched for graces that will accord with his manner: his teeth emerge, glistening with assimilated wit and sexual vitality. In

[4] *Ibid.*, I, 5.

Tolstoy's *Anna Karenina* Vronsky is another man with fine teeth, and they are part of that splendid animal, so much in love with his own body, that Vronsky even at best largely remains. They are an aspect of Vronsky's limiting, if radiant, physicality, related to his love of the regiment, of St. Petersburg society, of social as well as athletic games. For Henry Crawford the teeth are of less import; they are part of the hastily devised blazon of masculine charms the sisters require to adapt him to their narcissistic version of the future.

What this encounter, like every other, reveals is the movement toward specification. E. H. Gombrich has described brilliantly, through the analogy of the hobby-horse, the way in which a sense of relevance governs our search for attributes, in fact constitutes the forms we ascribe to things or people. The hobby-horse begins as a broomstick that a child uses as a substitute for a horse. Having found that he can use it for riding, he may project into it other attributes of horsiness—give it a tail, ears, a mane, perhaps a saddle. The child has begun with what we might call the generalized form of a horse; he specifies it more and more as its functions are called forth in play. Is this a representation of a horse? Or rather a substitute for one? The moral of Gombrich's fable is that "substitution may precede portrayal, and creation communication." [5] We work out from needs and we use substitute objects to satisfy them; we project upon those objects the attributes that new needs require.

What does Gombrich's hobby-horse tell us about the novel? First, it reminds us that the representation of fictional reality may grow out of conventional or archetypal forms, whether we see them as projections, as forms of play, or as models for

[5] Ernst H. Gombrich, *Meditations on a Hobby Horse and Other Essays on the Theory of Art* (London, 1963), p. 5.

control. They may acquire more and more differentiation as the images become actors in myths and the myths are adapted to our local anxieties or desires. Even more, Gombrich's analogy can show us that the elaborate forms of realism are generated less by the desire to represent the actual than by the pressure of conventions reaching outward for more complex differentiation. George Eliot, in the famous seventeenth chapter of *Adam Bede*, renounces the easy fictions of romance for the more difficult truths of realism. By this she means an extension of the conventions of romance into a realm where plots are bent to absorb the actualities of historic life, where the traditional characters are bleached and thickened until they become our colorless and undistinguished neighbors. George Eliot is not offering to give us a literal picture of social reality but to "give a faithful account of men and things as they have mirrored themselves in my mind." [6] This in fact becomes an extension of high forms to include the subliterary, even the antiliterary, details of a "monotonous homely existence." The "exact likeness" is the limiting point of the entire process whereby the generalized form is differentiated so sharply as to direct our feeling where it does not normally flow, so that it does not need to "wait for beauty" but "flows with resistless force and brings beauty with it." She sacrifices proportion and the "divine beauty of form" so as to extend art, as the Dutch painters had, to "those rounded backs and stupid weather-beaten faces that have bent over the spade and done the rough work of the world." The point I would stress is the deliberate —even militant—extension of forms rather than the effort at literal representation or record.

So in the encounter I have cited from Jane Austen there is a generalized image, cast in social terms, then specified in various

[6] Cf. Darrel Mansell, Jr., "Ruskin and George Eliot's 'Realism,'" *Criticism*, VII (1965), 203–16.

ways by observers. How far this specification is carried will depend on the character who observes or on the governing themes of the novelist. There are certain attributes that Jane Austen requires for her conception of reality, others that would distract or confuse us in following her kind of action. As Gombrich says, "If the hobby-horse became too lifelike, it might gallop away on its own." [7] To take this view of the novel is to see relevance itself expanding to require new detail, and the irrelevant detail becomes the boundary at the limit of expansion.

In *The Sense of an Ending*, Frank Kermode draws a sharp distinction between the simplicity of myths and the complexity of fictions, between wishful pattern and the skeptical testing of that pattern against the contingencies of the actual. Only in such testing can myths be disconfirmed, and the result of such disconfirmation will be those reversals or peripeties Aristotle finds in complex plots. The need to readjust expectations earns the mature fiction that incorporates contingencies without despairing of form. The myths of which Mr. Kermode writes—and there are some who would call them by a less cherished name—have often been adapted wishfully and conventionally to the more familiar situations of contemporary life, converting archetype into stereotype. It is these generalized forms with which the realistic novel always quarrels, breaking their limits by extension and insisting upon the stubbornness of the actual.[8]

In *Anna Karenina*, Tolstoy gives an account of the artistic

[7] Gombrich, *Meditations*, p. 8.

[8] *The Sense of an Ending* (New York, 1966). For criticism of Kermode's use of the term "myth," see Warner Berthoff, "Fiction, History, Myth: Notes toward the Discrimination of Narrative Form," in *The Interpretation of Narrative: Theory and Practice*, Harvard English Studies I, ed. Morton W. Bloomfield (Cambridge, Mass., 1970), pp. 263–87.

process that confirms this view. Mikhailov, the painter, is making a "sketch of a figure of a man in a fit of anger." The paper on which he is working is spotted with candle grease, and the grease spot suggests a new pose for the figure:

He was drawing this new pose when he suddenly remembered the energetic face, with a jutting-out chin, of a shopkeeper from whom he bought cigars, and he gave the man he was drawing that shopkeeper's face and chin. He laughed with delight. The figure he was drawing, instead of being dead and artificial, had sprung to life and could not possibly be altered. It was alive and was clearly and unmistakeably defined. The drawing could be corrected in accordance with the requirements of the figure; one could, and indeed one should, find a different position for the legs, change completely the position of the left arm, and throw back the hair. But in making these changes he did not alter the figure, but merely removed what concealed it. He merely removed, as it were, the coverings which made it impossible to see it; each new stroke revealed more and more the whole figure in all its force and vigor as it had suddenly appeared to him by the action of the grease spot.[9]

We may notice the stress first on the generalized form of an angry man, then the arbitrary suggestion in the form of the grease spot, the outward drive of an inner content or vision that seizes upon actual details of any sort to find specification, most of all the "force and vigor" of the conception that must be adequately embodied. Most interesting is the simultaneous sense of embodiment and of revelation. Once the artist finds, through contingency, a necessary outward form, that form must in turn be protected from, stripped free of, the merely

[9] *Anna Karenina*, Part V, Ch. 10, trans. David Magarshack (New York, 1961), pp. 472–73.

habitual or trivial irrelevancy. This double aspect of the concrete detail—at once a condition of revelation and a threat of irrelevancy—is crucial.

At what point does the covering achieve full opacity? Virginia Woolf, in her famous essay "Mr. Bennett and Mrs. Brown," warns against the reliance on mere social convention. She imagines the English public speaking:

Old women have houses. They have fathers. They have incomes. They have servants. They have hot-water bottles. That is how we know that they are old women. Mr. Wells and Mr. Bennett and Mr. Galsworthy have always taught us that this is the way to recognize them.

The Georgian novelists "have given us a house in the hope that we may be able to deduce the human beings who live there." In contrast, Mrs. Woolf defends "an old lady of unlimited capacity and infinite variety; capable of appearing in any place; wearing any dress; saying anything and doing heaven knows what." [10]

Any dress? Why then should we learn that Emma Bovary, when she first appears to Charles, wears a dress of blue merino wool with flounces? [11] Emma's dress is no more a thing than a statement, no more a covering than a revelation. The fine wool, the romantic blue of Emma's fantasies, the flounces that contrast with the farmhouse but accord with its self-indulgent luxuries—all these are intimations of Emma's nature and also, for Charles Bovary, intimations of a life of the senses such as he has never known. The details of Emma's dress are not mere

[10] "Mr. Bennett and Mrs. Brown" (1924), in *Collected Essays* (London, 1966), I, 333, 336-37.

[11] *Madame Bovary*, I, ii ("en robe de mérinos bleu garnie de trois volants").

social forms, although they include them. They mark the convergence of several themes, not all of them fully established as yet in the narrative. Their meaning catches at once something of Emma's temperament and Charles's, something of the economic pattern that will mark her career, something of the incongruity Flaubert will exploit so elaborately in the scenes of the agricultural fair. The details avoid the telltale simplification of the smart novelist with a so-called eye for detail, where the detail tends to make a strong and simple sociological assertion. Emma's dress is full of implication, some of it only retrospectively clear; but there is no suspension of narrative movement to permit it, as it were, to make its assertion, nor is there that discontinuity of literal narrative that marks the intervention of a symbol.

How, then, does the novelist prevent these objects, the conditions of plausible actuality, from becoming mere covering? How does he preserve the function of the actual as a language, that is, as relevance? This may be done in part by the presence of a narrator, commenting upon events as George Eliot does, generalizing their import, serving as a reminder and model of the whole process of translation of object into statement. Without such a narrator, there is the effect of ordonnance, of clear artifice of arrangement, of cumulative repetition. Of *Anna Karenina* Tolstoy wrote in a letter:

. . . if the shortsighted critics think that I merely wanted to describe what appealed to me, such as the sort of dinner Oblonsky has or what Anna's shoulders are like, then they are mistaken. In everything . . . I wrote I was guided by the need of collecting ideas which, linked together, would be the expression of myself, though each individual idea, expressed separately in words, loses its meaning; is horribly debased when only one of the links, of which it forms a part, is taken by itself. But the interlinking of these ideas is not, I think, an intellectual process, but something else, and it is impossible to express the source of this interlinking directly in words; it can only be done indirectly by describing images, actions, and situations in words.[12]

Those linkages reveal, as fully as the most eloquent narrator, the control of the author and the bold use of pattern. We can see one instance when Levin comes to visit his old friend Stiva Oblonsky. Levin has come to propose to Kitty; Stiva and Kitty's older sister Dolly are estranged since she has discovered his affair with a French governess. Levin calls on Oblonsky at his office, where we see Oblonsky's remarkable tact and charm as a bureaucrat, and they meet again for dinner. As they enter the restaurant there is a "sort of suppressed raidance" on Oblonsky's face; he gives his order to the Tartar waiter, he jokes with the painted French woman at the cashier's desk. Levin tries to guard his own idealized vision of Kitty in this place of unclean sensuality.

They are greeted by a "particularly obsequious white-headed old Tartar [waiter] so broad across the hips that the tails of his coat did not meet." The waiter allows Oblonsky to order in Russian but repeats the name of each dish in French, hurries off with coattails flying, and "five minutes later rushes in again with a dish of oysters, their pearly shells open, and a bottle between his fingers." Once he has poured the wine, the

[12] Letter to N. N. Strakhov, April 23 and 26, 1876 (original in Jubilee Edition, *Polnoe Sobranie Sochinenii* [Moscow, 1928–58], LXII, 268–70), here cited from the Foreword to David Magarshack's translation of *Anna Karenina* (cited above), pp. xii–xiii. For an alternative translation of a portion and a discussion of *svyazi* (links, ties) or *stsepleniya* (couplings, connections), see R. F. Christian, *Tolstoy's "War and Peace": A Study* (Oxford, 1962), pp. 123–24.

fat old waiter looks at Oblonsky "with a smile of undisguised
pleasure." For Levin, "this continuous bustle of running about,
these bronzes, mirrors, gaslights, Tartars—all this seemed an
affront. . . . He was afraid of besmirching that which filled his
soul." But Levin can only remark aloud on the difference from
meals in the country, got over as quickly as possible so as to
return to work—whereas here, in Moscow, "you and I are
doing our best to make our dinner last as long as possible and
for that reason have oysters." When Oblonsky replies, "That's
the whole aim of civilization: to make everything a source of
enjoyment," Levin's response is simply, "Well, if that is so, I'd
rather be a savage." [13]

Somewhat later they discuss Oblonsky's affair with the governess. Levin is incredulous and unsympathetic; he refuses Oblonsky the comfortable pathos of seeing love as a tragic dilemma. And Oblonsky replies coolly:

. . . you are a thoroughly earnest and sincere man. That is
your strength and your limitation. You are thoroughly earnest
and sincere and you want all life to be earnest and sincere too,
but it never is. You despise public service because you think its
practice ought to be as singleminded as its aims, but that never
happens. You want the activity of every single man always to
have an aim, and love and family life always to be one and the
same thing. But that doesn't happen either. All the diversity,
all the charm, all the beauty of life are made up of light and
shade.

Then Tolstoy gives us one of his moments of ironic
omniscience:

And suddenly both felt that, though they were friends and
had dined and wined together, which should have drawn them

[13] *Anna Karenina*, Part I, Ch. 10.

closer, each was thinking only of his own affairs and was not really concerned with the other.

Tolstoy has made the dinner, which occurs early in the novel, the basis of many of the linkages that will run through the book—most essentially the linkages of those who, with varying degrees of awareness and self-acceptance, take an aesthetic view of life and those who, with all the strain and quixotic intensity it may involve, take an ethical view. In Oblonsky's grace and tact, his contentment in the shallow waters that are secure and comfortably warm, we see aspects of Vronsky as well. In Levin's intransigent need to commit himself totally and to exact a meaning for his life we see the heroic possibilities, so cruelly unrealized, of Anna herself. The fat and obsequious old Tartar waiter fills out the scene of such a restaurant as Oblonsky would frequent, but he is also a striking statement of the irreducible hedonism that underlies the aesthetic vision of the beauty of life made up of light and shade.

There is a border area where details are pulled between the demands of structure and the consistent texture of a plausible fictional world. Their nature is not unlike those details of our own lives that are jointly to be explained by outward circumstance and inward motive. Each of us is thrown into a world he never made, and yet each of us makes of it what he must. At some level of conscious or unconscious action we choose ourselves and our world. One of the dazzling and perhaps terrifying aspects of Freud's vision is that it seems everywhere to supplant chance by choice, to shackle accidents in the tracing of purposiveness. It does not preclude contingencies, for it cannot determine what will enter into our experience, but it can show the way we use and shape that experience.

The analogy for the novel is the measure of relevance it may confer upon the most peripheral and accidental detail. Yet to live in a state of unrelieved and intense relevance is something like paranoia, a condition of lucid and overdeterminate design. Such a vision imposes its design at every point, obsessively and repetitiously. The design is everywhere present and everywhere visible. The novel gives us instead the complex awareness of seeing the tough opacity of the actual and at the same time seeing it as a radiant construction of meaning. To get at how this is done requires that we consider for a moment the famous gestalt figure of the duck-rabbit. The same drawing accommodates either image and can be read as either, but it cannot be read simultaneously as both. It is related to those subtler ambiguities of form that we see in puzzles of figure and ground. The figure, if it is given sharp enough definition, will always seek to constitute itself against the interruption of another form; it will seem to thrust the other form back into third-dimensional space as a ground. So long as there is greater definition or familiarity in one form, it will prevail in our perception as figure. These puzzles of perception give us a hint about the structure of novels.[14]

The openings of novels serve to set the rules of the game to be played by the reader. The degree of specification in setting, the presence or absence of a persona behind the narrative voice, the verbal density of the style—its metaphorical elaboration or cultivated innocence—all these are ways of indicating the nature of the game, of educating the responses and guiding the collaboration of the reader. If a novel moves

[14] On figure and ground, see Rudolf Arnheim, *Art and Visual Perception* (Berkeley and Los Angeles, 1954), pp. 177–85, 198–203. The analogy introduces spatial terms that may be misleading, but it catches better than any other I know the shifting structure of the field of our attention, and, by implication, the shifting function of elements of the novel.

through disjunct sets of characters in successive chapters, we are teased with the problem of how they shall be connected —by the working of the plot (like Esther Summerson and Lady Dedlock) or by thematic analogy (like Clarissa Dalloway and Septimus Smith). But once the novel enters into full narrative movement, the problem of how it shall be read becomes a matter of less immediate concern or full attention. Once its premises are given, the world of the novel becomes the scene of an action, and our commitment to the narrative movement tends to absorb our attention. Narrative may be said to depress the metaphorical status of character and setting; it gives a coherence to all the elements on the level of action that deflects attention from their meaningfulness and from their position in the structure. One can see something very much like this in pictorial representation. The use of perspective makes us read each detail of a painting as it might relate in space to every other detail in a three-dimensional "virtual world." It will require a very strong linear pattern or color relationship to win our attention once more to the flat surface from which we have imaginatively departed.

The narrative movement, with its strong temporal flow and its stress upon causal sequence, may compel full attention to itself. The setting becomes the necessary ground of the action, the characters the necessary agent. But shifts from figure to ground may be instantaneous and, where both figure and ground are more complex, far less dramatic than in the didactic example of the duck-rabbit. At moments the causal sequence moves entirely within the consciousness of the principal character, and the external action becomes the ground against which character is displayed.

Let us consider a sequence of such moments in *Anna Karenina*. First there is the instance of the mowers. Levin has been

troubled by the difficulty of persuading the peasants to accept
his agricultural programs. He is more immediately oppressed
by the skeptical condescension of his half-brother, the intellectual Koznyshev, who always has the power to shake or completely undo Levin's convictions. Levin decides to join the
peasants in order to escape from thought and from the frustrations of self-consciousness.

The longer Levin went on mowing, the oftener he experienced
those moments of oblivion when it was not that his arms
swung the scythe, but that the scythe itself made his whole
body, full of life and conscious of itself, move after it, and as
though by magic the work did itself, of its own accord and
without a thought being given to it, with the utmost precision
and regularity. Those were the most blessed moments.[15]

As he joins the workers at dinner time, all constraint between
them vanishes, but when Levin returns home, his brother's
condescension resumes. Koznyshev is filled with the well-being
of having solved two chess problems, and Levin must find a
pretext for escape so that he can guard his own memory of
communion and of blissful self-transcendence.

These moments of oblivion recur in the novel; they accompany the death of Levin's brother and the birth of his son:

But both that sorrow and this joy were equally beyond the ordinary conditions of life. In this ordinary life they were like
openings through which something higher became visible.
And what was happening now was equally hard and agonizing
to bear and equally incomprehensible, and one's soul, when
contemplating it, soared to a height such as one did not think
possible before and where reason could not keep up with it.[16]

[15] *Anna Karenina*, Part III, Ch. 5.   [16] *Ibid*., Part VII, Ch. 14.

It is at these moments that the events of Levin's life, his long quixotic career of experiment and debate, come to their fullest intensity. These are moments where all the action passes into the shaping of a self and the outward action gives way to internal dialectic. As it does at the very close.

I shall still get angry with my coachman Ivan, I shall still argue and express my thoughts inopportunely; there will still be a wall between the holy of holies of my soul and other people, even my wife, and I shall still blame her for my own fears and shall regret it; I shall still be unable to understand with my reason why I am praying, and I shall continue to pray— but my life, my whole life, independently of anything that may happen to me, every moment of it, is no longer meaningless as it was before, but has an incontestable meaning of goodness, with which I have the power to invest it.[17]

At the close of the novel Levin at last achieves a fusion of temporal movement with the sense of meaningfulness that has marked these moments of oblivion, of temporal arrest. For it is meaningfulness more than timelessness that matters; the arrest of time is the intimation of meaning, a sudden ascent above the stream of events and the uncertainties that beset him so long as he remains immersed in that stream. For Levin these moments are a freedom from the conditional, the determined, the horizontal flow of time.

This slipping in and out of time, from surges of doubt and perplexity to moments of arresting meaningfulness, is comparable to shifts in our process of reading the novel. We move from the temporal action to moments where character subsumes action, where ground shifts to figure. So too we move, in a more general way, from the flow of temporal succession

[17] *Ibid.*, Part VIII, Ch. 19.

to a pattern that might be called spatial, where the recognition
of relevance leaps to the center of attention and displaces the
narrative sequence or the imagined world. The very repetition
of this pattern of moments of oblivion and transcendence is
one way in which Tolstoy's novel calls attention to the full dimensions of Levin's being, to the elements of his character that
are absent from Oblonsky's. The intensity with which Levin
encounters these moments is placed in contrast with Oblonsky's equable and conscienceless hedonism. To say "placed in
contrast" is perhaps to beg the question, but a spatial metaphor
is hard to avoid.

As critics have often observed, to speak of temporal and spatial forms is at best to use imperfect analogies. "Temporal
form" stresses the ongoing movement and irreversible direction
of narrative; "spatial form," the simultaneity of presentation
that a painting allows. We study the painting through time
and apprehend its various relationships of line and color successively, but we can see them presented before us at once.
Some have preferred the metaphor of musicalization to spatiali-
zation. It does justice to temporal movement, and it stresses, as
does the spatial metaphor, a structural pattern that can be
schematically represented. What is at stake, clearly, is neither
space nor time but the awareness of structure that relates elements in all parts of the book. One may confuse matters by
evoking a new metaphor. I derive it from Roger Fry's account
of a Sung bowl, written out of no concern with literary analogy and therefore all the more useful:

. . . we apprehend gradually the shape of the outside contour,
the perfect sequence of the curves, and the subtle modifications of a certain type of curve which it shows; we also feel
the relation of the concave curves of the inside to the outside
contour; we realize that the precise thickness of the walls is

consistent with the particular kind of matter of which it is made, its appearance of density and resistance; and finally we recognize, perhaps, how satisfactory for the display of all these plastic qualities are the color and the dull luster of the glaze. Now while we are thus occupied there comes to us, I think, a feeling of purpose; we feel that all these sensually logical conformities are the outcome of a particular feeling, or of what, for want of a better word, we call an idea; and we may even say that the pot is the expression of an idea in the artist's mind. Whether we are right or not in making this deduction, I believe it nearly always occurs in such esthetic apprehension of an object of art.[18]

Fry's bowl has its various aspects, each of them apprehended in itself and yet all related by an idea, a purposiveness that can account for the simultaneous accommodation of diverse elements and functions in a single structure. We can attend to the glaze of the bowl quite apart from its form; we can see the exterior outline without relating it to the inner curve; we can see the bowl as a structure without much concern for its function. And yet we cannot quite do any of these things in isolation. Each may become momentarily the center of our attention, but there is always some latent awareness of the interrelatedness of all these aspects.

It is through this analogy that I would return to the irrelevant detail. It is not, of course, irrelevant, but it has so attenuated and complex a relevance as to confirm rather than directly to assert a meaning. Its meaningfulness, in fact, may become fully apparent only as the total structure emerges. It serves meanwhile a sufficient function in sustaining the virtual world in which the structure is embodied. One can say that its

[18] Roger Fry, "The Artist's Vision" (1919), in *Vision and Design* (London, 1920), pp. 32 f.

particularity is all that we are required to observe in its immediate configuration; yet only so much particularity is created
as is consonant with that conceptual force the detail acquires
in the large structure. The local configuration, then, has the
potential lucidity of a model and the actual density of an
event.

Roland Barthes has tried to isolate the detail which has no
conceivable relevance, which seems mere arbitrary fact or
event, "neither incongruous nor significant." He takes such a
detail to have as its function the very assertion that it is the
real; what it signifies is the category of the real itself.[19] This is
ingenious but hardly satisfactory. Even if we take it as a theoretical distinction which need not occur to us in the process of
reading, it still seems to rest upon an ambiguous and sliding
use of "signification." If one imagines a family reunion where
all degrees of kinship are represented and one or two people
attend whose kinship cannot be clearly established at all, shall

[19] "L'Effet du Réel," *Communications*, No. 11 (1969), pp. 84–89.
M. Barthes cites as one illustration the description of Mme Au-
bain's household in *Un Coeur Simple:* "un vieux piano supportait,
sous un baromètre, un tas pyramidal de boîtes et de cartons." The
piano, he suggests, may imply middle-class standing, the heap of
boxes the disorder of the household. But the barometer has no
such function, however indirect, to account for it.

If M. Barthes means, most generally, that realism involves a superfluity of detail, that is, some details which exceed any structural
pattern of meaning and therefore any possible relevance, I should
question the point. The effect of the real does not depend upon
superfluity of detail but rather upon the kind of detail that is provided. The barometer is an object of a certain kind: practical, useful, prosaic. But so are the boxes heaped on the piano, and, whatever they suggest of disorder, they serve no less than the
barometer to assert the real. So, too, with the Tartar waiter cited
above from *Anna Karenina:* he acquires significance through linkages, but he is at the same time a portion of a circumstantial
world presented in terms that do not insist upon its significance.

we say of the one or two that they represent the human family or the community of mankind? This is to extend the idea of kinship to a point where it becomes an equivocation, and something of the sort occurs in Barthes's treatment of the irrelevant detail. We may claim that these limiting cases—of kinship or of relevance—awaken our consciousness of what it is that relates all these elements. But the limiting case does so through its very incongruity. It does not signify as other instances signify; it violates the rules of a language game and makes us aware of the game itself. Yet Barthes does not claim so much for the details he cites, nor is this our experience in reading the works he cites.

It is not a flounce or a barometer that alone asserts the real; all the details together make that assertion, and all are potentially significant as well. Details do not offer themselves as clearly relevant or irrelevant. It is only the special case where the detail insists upon its relevance or, as it may in some versions of surrealism or of the absurd, upon its irrelevance. Even if, in retrospective analysis, we see certain details as limiting cases of relevance, we can hardly separate them from that dense tissue of events out of which the structure emerges. For that emergence is always imperfect and incomplete. The full import of any detail remains a problem at best, just as does the structural form itself. We may achieve approximations in either case, but we may easily force meanings by distortion of emphasis or failure of tact. The elements of a novel shift in function, I have tried to show, as the work unfolds and as new linkages are revealed. For this reason we can never with confidence ascribe a single purpose or meaning to a detail, nor can we give an exhaustive reading of the structure.

Let me illustrate this with a final example, one drawn from Dickens's *Bleak House*. In the neighborhood of Chancery we

encounter the deaths of Captain Hawdon, the lover of Lady
Dedlock and the father of Esther Summerson, and of his drunk-
en landlord, Krook. On both occasions we study the responses in Chancery Lane and especially in the nearby pub,
the Sol's Arms:

. . . where the sound of the piano through the partly-opened
windows jingles out into the court, and where Little Swills,
after keeping the lovers of harmony in a roar like a very Yor-
ick, may now be heard taking the gruff line in a concerted
piece, and sentimentally adjuring his friends and patrons to
Listen, listen, listen, Tew the wa-ter-Fall! Mrs. Perkins and
Mrs. Piper compare opinions on the subject of the young lady
of professional celebrity who assists at the Harmonic Meetings,
and who has a space to herself in the manuscript announce-
ment in the window; Mrs. Perkins possessing information that
she has been married a year and a half, though announced as
Miss M. Melvilleson, the noted syren, and that her baby is
clandestinely conveyed to the Sol's Arms every night to receive its natural nourishment during the entertainments.
"Sooner than which, myself," says Mrs. Perkins, "I would get
my living by selling lucifers." Mrs. Piper, as in duty bound, is
of the same opinion; holding that a private station is better
than public applause, and thanking Heaven for her own (and,
by implication, Mrs. Perkins's) respectability. By this time, the
potboy of the Sol's Arms appearing with her supperpint well
frothed, Mrs. Piper accepts that tankard and retires in-doors,
first giving a fair good-night to Mrs. Perkins, who has had her
own pint in her hand ever since it was fetched from the same
hostelry by young Perkins before he was sent to bed.[20]

Little Swills, Mrs. Perkins, Mrs. Piper, and the suspect Miss
M. Melvilleson have no conceivable relation to Dickens's plot,

[20] *Bleak House*, Ch. 32.

and this alone is a distinction in a book so elaborately contrived. Yet there they are, enormously lively and entertaining, insisting on the stability of a world that may also contain the outrageous and terrible. They are there and, being there, they demand a share in the structure of the book. To call them ground is not to absolve them of meaning, for ground and figure interlock at least through significant contrast. They may be reminiscent of that rougher texture at the lower part of the statue or the building, at once an element of the design and yet a vestige of the resistant materials from which the work was fashioned. They are not to be put by entirely; if they contribute to the condition of illusion or testify to the real, they also budge somewhat the inner meaning or structure of the work. It must be extended, however slightly, to admit their presence. So long as they have this power, the meaning remains always in process, the form always emerging.

 Gérard Genette

TIME AND NARRATIVE IN
A la recherche du temps perdu

I suggest a study of *narrative discourse* or, in a slightly different formulation, of *narrative (récit) as discourse (discours)*. As a point of departure, let us accept the hypothesis that all narratives, regardless of their complexity or degree of elaboration—and Proust's *A la recherche du temps perdu*, the text I shall be using as an example, reaches of couse a very high degree of elaboration—can always be considered to be the development of a verbal statement such as "I am walking," or "He will come," or "Marcel becomes a writer." On the strength of this rudimentary analogy, the problems of narrative discourse can be classified under three main headings: the categories of *time* (temporal relationships between the narrative [story] and the "actual" events that are being told [history]); of *mode* (relationships determined by the distance and perspective of the narrative with respect to the history); and of *voice* (relationships between the narrative and the narrating agency itself: narrative situation, level of narration, status of the narrator and of the recipient, etc.). I shall deal only, and very sketchily, with the first category.

The time-category can itself be divided into three sections: the first concerned with the relationships between the temporal *order* of the events that are being told and the pseudo-temporal order of the narrative; the second concerned with the relationships between the *duration* of the events and the duration of the narrative; the third dealing with relationships of *frequency* of repetition between the events and the narrative, between history and story.

ORDER

It is well known that the folk-tale generally keeps a one-to-one correspondence between the "real" order of events that are being told and the order of the narrative, whereas literary narrative, from its earliest beginnings in Western literature, that is, in the Homeric epic, prefers to use the beginning *in medias res*, generally followed by an explanatory flashback. This chronological reversal has become one of the formal *topoi* of the epic genre. The style of the novel has remained remarkably close to its distant origin in this respect: certain beginnings in Balzac, as in the *Duchesse de Langeais* or *César Birotteau*, immediately come to mind as typical examples.

From this point of view, the *Recherche*—especially the earlier sections of the book—indicates that Proust made a much more extensive use than any of his predecessors of his freedom to reorder the temporality of events.

The first "time," dealt with in the six opening pages of the book, refers to a moment that cannot be dated with precision but that must take place quite late in the life of the protagonist: the time at which Marcel, during a period when, as he says, "he often used to go to bed early," suffered from spells of insomnia during which he relived his own past. The first moment in the organization of the narrative is thus far from being the first in the order of the reported history, which deals with the life of the hero.

The second moment refers to the memory relived by the protagonist during his sleepless night. It deals with his child-hood at Combray, or, more accurately, with a specific but par-ticularly important moment of this childhood: the famous scene that Marcel calls "the drama of his going to bed," when his mother, at first prevented by Swann's visit from giving him his ritualistic good-night kiss, finally gives in and consents to spend the night in his room.

The third moment again moves far ahead, probably to well within the period of insomnia referred to at the start, or a little after the end of this period: it is the episode of the *madeleine*, during which Marcel recovers an entire fragment of his child-hood that had up till then remained hidden in oblivion.

This very brief third episode is followed at once by a fourth: a second return to Combray, this time much more ex-tensive than the first in temporal terms since it covers the en-tire span of the Combray childhood. Time segment (4) is thus contemporary with time segment (2) but has a much more ex-tensive duration.

The fifth moment is a very brief return to the initial state of sleeplessness and leads to a new retrospective section that takes us even further back into the past, since it deals with a love ex-perience of Swann that took place well before the narrator was born.

There follows a seventh episode that occurs some time after the last events told in the fourth section (childhood at Com-

bray): the story of Marcel's adolescence in Paris and of his
love for Gilberte. From then on, the story will proceed in
more closely chronological order, at least in its main articulations.

A la recherche du temps perdu thus begins with a zigzag-
ging movement that could easily be represented by a graph
and in which the relationship between the time of events and
the time of the narrative could be summarized as follows:
N(arrative) $1 = $ H(istory) 4; $N_2 = H_2$; $N_3 = H_4$; $N_4 = H_2$;
$N_5 = H_4$; $N_6 = H_1$ (Swann's love); $N_7 = H_3$. We are clearly
dealing with a highly complex and deliberate transgression of
chronological order. I have said that the rest of the book follows a more continuous chronology in its main patterns, but
this large-scale linearity does not exclude the presence of a
great number of anachronisms in the details: *retrospections*, as
when the story of Marcel's stay in Paris during the year 1914
is told in the middle of his later visit to Paris during 1916; or
anticipations, as when, in the last pages of *Du Côté de chez
Swann*, Marcel describes what has become of the Bois de
Boulogne at a much later date, the very year he is actually
engaged in writing his book. The transition from the *Côté des
Guermantes* to *Sodome et Gomorrhe* is based on an interplay of
anachronisms: the last scene of *Guermantes* (announcing the
death of Swann) in fact takes place later than the subsequent
first scene of *Sodome* (the meeting between Charlus and Ju-
pien).

I do not intend to analyze the narrative anachronisms in detail but will point out in passing that one should distinguish
between *external* and *internal* anachronisms, according to
whether they are located without or within the limits of the
temporal field defined by the main narrative. The external anachronisms raise no difficulty, since there is no danger that they

will interfere with the main narrative. The internal anachronisms, on the contrary, create a problem of interference. So we must subdivise them into two groups, according to the nature of this relation. Some function to fill in a previous or later blank (ellipsis) in the narrative and can be called *completive* anachronisms, such as the retrospective story of Swann's death. Others return to a moment that has already been covered in the narrative: they are *repetitive* or apparently redundant anachronisms but fulfill in fact a very important function in the organization of the novel. They function as *announcements* (in the case of prospective anticipations) or as *recalls* (when they are retrospective). Announcements can, for example, alert the reader to the meaning of a certain event that will only later be fully revealed (as with the lesbian scene at Montjouvain that will later determine Marcel's jealous passion for Albertine). Recalls serve to give a subsequent meaning to an event first reported as without particular significance (as when we find that Albertine's belated response to a knock on the door was caused by the fact that she had locked herself in with Andrée), or serve even more often to alter the original meaning—as when Marcel discovers after more than thirty years' time that Gilberte was in love with him at Combray and that what he took to be a gesture of insolent disdain was actually meant to be an advance.

Next to these relatively simple and unambiguous retrospections and anticipations, one finds more complex and ambivalent forms of anachronisms: anticipations within retrospections, as when Marcel remembers what used to be his projects with regard to the moment that he is now experiencing; retrospections within anticipations, as when the narrator indicates how he will later find out about the episode he is now in the process of telling; "announcements" of events that have already

been told anticipatively or "recalls" of events that took place
earlier in the story but that have not yet been told; retrospections that merge seamlessly with the main narrative and make
it impossible to identify the exact status of a given section, etc.
Finally, I should mention what is perhaps the rarest but most
specific of all instances: structures that could properly be
called *achronisms*, that is to say, episodes entirely cut loose
from any chronological situation whatsoever. These occurrences were pointed out by J. P. Houston in a very interesting
study published in *French Studies*, January, 1962, entitled
"Temporal Patterns in *À la recherche du temps perdu*." Near
the end of *Sodome et Gomorrhe*, as Marcel's second stay at
Balbec draws to a close, Proust tells a sequence of episodes not
in the order in which they took place but by following the
succession of roadside-stops made by the little train on its journey from Balbec to La Raspelière. Events here follow a geo-
graphical rather than a chronological pattern. It is true that
the sequence of places still depends on a temporal event (the
journey of the train), but this temporality is not that of the
"real" succession of events. A similar effect is achieved in the
composition of the end of *Combray*, when the narrator successively describes a number of events that took place on the
Méséglise way, at different moments, by following the order of
their increasing distance from Combray. He follows the temporal succession of a walk from Combray to Méséglise and
then, after returning to his spatial and temporal point of departure, tells a sequence of events that took place on the Guermantes way using exactly the same principle. The temporal
order of the narrative is not that of the actual succession of
events, unless it happens to coincide by chance with the sequence of places encountered in the course of the walk.

I have given some instances of the freedom that Proust's narrative takes with the chronological order of events, but such a description is necessarily sketchy and even misleading if other elements of narrative temporality such as duration and frequency are not also taken into account.

DURATION

Generally speaking, the idea of an isochrony between narrative and "history" is highly ambiguous, for the narrative unit which, in literature, is almost always a narrative text cannot really be said to possess a definite duration. One could equate the duration of a narrative with the time it takes to read it, but reading-times vary considerably from reader to reader, and an ideal average speed can only be determined by fictional means. It may be better to start out from a definition in the form of a relative quantity, and define isochrony as a uniform projection of historical time on narrative extension, that is, number of pages per duration of event. In this way, one can record variations in the speed of the narrative in relation to itself and measure effects of acceleration, deceleration, stasis, and ellipsis (blank spaces within the narrative while the flow of events keeps unfolding).

I have made some rather primitive calculations of the relative speed of the main narrative articulations, measuring on the one hand the narrative of the *Recherche* by number of pages and on the other hand the events by quantity of time. Here are the results.

The first large section, *Combray* or Marcel's childhood, numbers approximately 180 pages of the Pléiade edition and covers about ten years (let me say once and for all that I am defining the duration of events by general consensus, knowing that it is open to question on several points). The next episode,

Swann's love-affair with Odette, uses approximately 200 pages to cover about two years. The Gilberte episode (end of *Swann*, beginning of *Jeunes filles en fleurs*) devotes 160 pages to a duration that can be evaluated at two or three years. Here we encounter an elipsis involving two years of the protagonist's life and mentioned in passing in a few words at the beginning of a sentence. The Balbec episode numbers 300 pages for a three-month-long time-span; then the lengthy section dealing with life in Paris society (*Côté de Guermantes* and beginning of *Sodome et Gomorrhe*) takes up 750 pages for two and a half years. It should be added that considerable variations occur within this section: 110 pages are devoted to the afternoon party at Mme de Villeparisis's that lasts for about two hours, 150 pages to the dinner of nearly equal length at the Duchesse de Guermantes's, and 100 pages to the evening at the Princesse de Guermantes's. In this vast episode of 750 pages for two and a half years, 360 pages—nearly one half—are taken up by less than ten hours of social life.

The second stay at Balbec (end of *Sodome*) covers approximately six months in 380 pages. Then the Albertine sequence, reporting the hero's involvement with Albertine in Paris (*La Prisonnière* and the beginning of *La Fugitive*), requires 630 pages for an eighteen-month period, of which 300 deal with only two days. The stay in Venice uses 35 pages for a few weeks, followed by a section of 40 pages (astride *La Fugitive* and *Le Temps retrouvé*) for the stay in Tansonville, the return to the country of Marcel's childhood. The first extended ellipsis of the *Recherche* occurs here; the time-span cannot be determined with precision, but it encompasses approximately ten years of the hero's life spent in a rest-home. The subsequent episode, situated during the war, devotes 130 pages to a few weeks, followed by another ellipsis of ten years again spent in a rest-home. Finally, the concluding scene, the party at the Princesse de Guermantes's, devotes 190 pages to a two- or three-hour-long reception.

What conclusions can be derived from this barren and apparently useless enumeration? First of all, we should note the extensive shifts in relative duration, ranging from one line of text for ten years to 190 pages for two or three hours, or from approximately one page per century to one page per minute. The second observation refers to the internal evolution of the *Recherche* as a whole. It could be roughly summarized by stressing, on the one hand, the gradual slowing down of the narrative achieved by the insertion of longer and longer scenes for events of shorter and shorter duration. This is compensated for, on the other hand, by the presence of more and more extensive ellipses. The two trends can be easily united in one formula: increasing discontinuity of the narrative. As the Proustian narrative moves toward its conclusion, it becomes increasingly discontinuous, consisting of gigantic scenes separated from each other by enormous gaps. It deviates more and more from the ideal "norm" of an isochronic narrative.

We should also stress how Proust selects among the traditional literary forms of narrative duration. Among the nearly infinite range of possible combinations of historical and narrative duration, the literary tradition has made a rather limited choice that can be reduced to the following fundamental forms: (1) the *summary*, when the narrative duration is greatly reduced with respect to the historical duration; it is well known that the summary constitutes the main connective tissue in the classical *récit*; (2) the dramatic *scene*, especially the dialogue, when narrative and historical time are supposed to be nearly equal; (3) the narrative *stasis*, when the narrative discourse continues while historical time is at a standstill, usually in order to take care of a description; and (4) *ellipsis*, consisting of a certain amount of historical time covered in a zero amount of narrative. If we consider the *Recherche* from this point of view, we are struck by the total absence of summarizing narrative, which tends to be absorbed in the ellipses, and by the near-total absence of descriptive stasis: the Proustian descriptions always correspond to an actual observation-time on the part of the character; the time-lapse is sometimes mentioned in the text and is obviously longer than the time it takes to read the description (three-quarters of an hour for the contemplation of the Elstir paintings owned by the Duc de Guermantes, when the description takes only four or five pages of the text). The narrative duration is not interrupted—as is so often the case with Balzac—for, rather than *describing*, Proust *narrates* how his hero perceives, contemplates, and experiences a given sight; the description is incorporated within the narrative and constitutes no autonomous narrative form. Except for another effect with which I shall deal at some length in a moment, Proust makes use of only two of the traditional forms of narrative duration: scene and ellipsis. And since ellipsis is a zero point of the text, we have in fact only one single form: the scene. I should add, however, without taking time to develop a rather obvious observation, that the narrative function of this traditional form is rather strongly subverted in Proust. The main number of his major scenes do not have the purely dramatic function usually associated with the classical "scene." The traditional economy of the novel, consisting of summarizing and nondramatic narrative alternating with dramatic scenes, is entirely discarded. Instead, we find another form of alternating movement toward which we must now direct our attention.

FREQUENCY

The third kind of narrative temporality, which has in general received much less critical and theoretical attention than the two previous ones, deals with the relative frequency of the narrated events and of the narrative sections that report them. Speaking once more very schematically, the most obvious form of narration will tell once what happens once, as in a narrative statement such as: "Yesterday, I went to bed early." This type of narrative is so current and presumably normal that it bears no special name. In order to emphasize that it is merely one possibility among many, I propose to give it a name and call it the *singulative* narrative (*récit singulatif*). It is equally possible to tell several times what happened several times, as when I say: "Monday I went to bed early, Tuesday I went to bed early, Wednesday I went to bed early," etc. This type of anaphoric narrative remains singulative and can be equated with the first, since the repetitions of the story correspond one-to-one to the repetitions of the events. A narrative can also tell several times, with or without variations, an event that happened only once, as in a statement of this kind: "Yesterday I went to bed early, yesterday I went to bed early, yesterday I tried to go to sleep well before dark," etc. This last hypothesis may seem *a priori* to be a gratuitous one, or even to exhibit a slight trace of senility. One should remember, however, that most texts by Alain Robbe-Grillet, among others, are founded on the repetitive potential of the narrative: the recurrent episode of the killing of the centipede, in *La Jalousie*, would be ample proof of this. I shall call *repetitive* narrative this type of narration, in which the story-repetitions exceed in number the repetitions of events. There remains a last possibility. Let us return to our second example: "Monday, Tuesday, Wednesday," etc. When such a pattern of events occurs, the narrative is obviously not reduced to the necessity of reproducing it as if its discourse were incapable of abstraction or synthesis. Unless a deliberate stylistic effect is aimed for, even the simplest narration will choose a formulation such as "every day" or "every day of the week" or "all week long." We all know which of these devices Proust chose for the opening sentence of the *Recherche*. The type of narrative in which a single narrative assertion covers several recurrences of the same event or, to be more precise, of several analogical events considered only with respect to what they have in common, I propose to call by the obvious name of *iterative* narrative (*récit itératif*).

My heavy-handed insistence on this notion may well seem out of place, since it designates a purely grammatical concept without literary relevance. Yet the quantitative amount and the qualitative function of the iterative mode are particularly important in Proust and have seldom, to my knowledge, received the critical attention they deserve. It can be said without exaggeration that the entire Combray episode is essentially an iterative narrative, interspersed here and there with some "singulative" scenes of salient importance such as the motherly good-night kiss, the meeting with the Lady in the pink dress (a retrospective scene), or the profanation of Vinteuil's portrait at Montjouvain. Except for five or six such scenes referring to a single action and told in the historical past (*passé défini*), all the rest, told in the imperfect, deals with what used to happen at Combray regularly, ritualistically, every night or every Sunday, or every Saturday, or whenever the weather was good or the weather was bad, etc. The narrative of Swann's love for Odette will still be conducted, for the most part, in the mode of habit and repetition; the same is true of the story of Marcel's love for Swann's daughter Gilberte. Only when we reach the stay at Balbec in the *Jeunes filles en fleurs* do the singulative episodes begin to predominate, although they remain interspersed with numerous iterative passages: the Balbec outings with Mme de Villeparisis and later with Albertine, the hero's stratagems at the beginning of *Guermantes* when he tries to meet the Duchess every morning, the journeys in the little train of the Raspelière (*Sodome*, II), life with Albertine in Paris (the first eighty pages of *La Prisonnière*) the walks in Venice (*La Fugitive*), not to mention the iterative treatment of certain moments within the singulative scenes, such as the conversations about genealogy during the dinner at the Duchess's, or the description of the aging guests at the last Guermantes party. The narrative synthesizes these moments by reducing several distinct occurrences to their common elements: "the *women* were like this . . . the *men* acted like that; *some* did this, *others* that," etc. I shall call these sections *internal iterations*, in contrast with other, more common passages, in which a descriptive-iterative parenthesis begins in the middle of a singulative scene to convey additional information needed for the reader's understanding and which I shall call *external iterations*. An example would be the long passage devoted, in the middle of the first Guermantes dinner, to the more general and therefore necessarily iterative description of the Guermantes wit.

The use of iterative narrative is by no means Proust's invention; it is one of the most classical devices of fictional narrative. But the frequency of the mode is distinctively Proustian, a fact still underscored by the relatively massive presence of what could be called *pseudo-iterations*, scenes presented (mostly by the use of the imperfect tense) as if they were iterative, but with such a wealth of precise detail that no reader can seriously believe that they could have taken place repeatedly in this way, without variations. One thinks for example of some of the conversations between Aunt Léonie and her maid Françoise that go on for page after page, or of conversations in Mme Verdurin's or Mme Swann's salon in Paris. In each of these cases, a singular scene has arbitrarily, and without any but grammatical change, been converted into an iterative scene, thus clearly revealing the trend of the Proustian narrative toward a kind of inflation of the iterative.

It would be tempting to interpret this tendency as symptomatic of a dominant psychological trait: Proust's highly developed sense of habit and repetition, his feeling for the *analogy* between different moments in life. This is all the more striking since the iterative mode of the narrative is not always, as in the Combray part, based on the repetitive, ritualistic pattern of a bourgeois existence in the provinces. Contrary to general belief, Proust is less aware of the specificity of moments than he is aware of the specificity of places; the latter is one of the governing laws of his sensibility. His moments have a strong tendency to blend into each other, a possibility which is at the root of the experience of spontaneous recollection. The opposition between the "singularity" of his spatial imagination and, if I dare say so, the "iterativity" of his temporal imagination is nicely illustrated in the following sentence from *Swann*. Speaking of the Guermantes landscape, Proust writes: "[Its] specificity would *at times*, in my dreams, seize upon me with almost fantastical power" ("le paysage dont *parfois*, la nuit dans mes rêves, l'individualité m'étreint avec une puissance presque fantastique"). Hence the highly developed sense of *ritual* (see, for example, the scene of the Saturday luncheons at Combray) and, on the other hand, the panic felt in the presence of irregularities of behavior, as when Marcel, at Balbec, wonders about the complex and secret law that may govern the unpredictable absences of the young girls on certain days.

But we must now abandon these psychological extrapolations and turn our attention to the technical questions raised by the iternative narration.

Every iterative sequence can be characterized by what may be called its *delimitation* and its *specification*. The delimitation determines the confines within the flow of external duration between which the iterative sequence, which generally has a beginning and an end, takes place. The delimitation can be vague, as when we are told that "from a certain year on, Mlle Vinteuil could never be seen alone" (I, 147), or precise, defined—a very rare occurrence in Proust—by a specific date, or by reference to a particular event, as when the break between Swann and the Verdurins puts an end to an iterative sequence telling of Swann's encounters with Odette and starts off a new sequence. The specification, on the other hand, points out the recurring periodicity of the iterative unit. It can be indefinite (as is frequently the case in Proust who introduces an iterative statement by such adverbs of time as "sometimes," "often," "on certain days," etc.) or definite, when it follows an absolute and regular pattern such as: "every day," "every Sunday," etc. The pattern can also be more irregular and relative, as when the walks toward Méséglise are said to take place in bad or uncertain weather, or the walks toward Guermantes whenever the weather is good. Two or more specifications can of course be juxtaposed. "Every summer" and "every Sunday" combine to give "every Sunday in the summer," which is the iterative specification of much of the Combray section.

The interplay between these two dimensions of the iterative

narrative varies and enriches a temporal mode threatened, by
its very nature, by a degree of abstraction. Provided it has a
certain length, an iterative section can very closely resemble an
ordinary narrative, except for some grammatical traits. Yet it
goes without saying that a narrative such as "Sunday at Combray" that would retain only events that *all* Sundays have in
common would run the risk of becoming as dryly schematic as
a stereotyped time-schedule. The monotony can be avoided by
playing on the internal delimitations and specifications.

Internal delimitations: for instance, the diachronic caesura
brought about by the story of the encounter with the "Lady
in the pink dress" in the narration of Marcel's Sunday afternoon readings: this encounter will bring about a change of locale,
after the quarrel between Marcel's parents and Uncle Adolphe
has put the latter's room out of bounds. Another instance
would be the change of direction in the hero's dreams of literary glory after his first encounter with the Duchess in the church
of Combray. The single scene, in those instances, divides
the iterative sequence into a *before* and an *after*, and so diversifies
it into two subsequences which function as two *variants*.

Internal specifications: I mentioned the good weather / bad
weather pattern which introduces a definite specification in the
iterative series of the Sunday walks and determines the choice
between Guermantes and Méséglise. Most of the time, however, the iterative narrative is diversified in indefinite specifications introduced by "sometimes . . ." or "one time . . . some
other time . . . ," etc. These devices allow for a very flexible
system of variations and for a high degree of particularization,
without leaving the iterative mode. A characteristic example of
this technique occurs toward the end of the *Jeunes filles en
fleurs* in a description of Albertine's face (I, 946–47). The iterative mode, indeed, applies just as well to the descriptive as

to the narrative passages; half of Proust's descriptions make use of this mode:

Certains jours, mince, le teint gris, l'air maussade, une transparence violette descendant obliquement au fond de ses yeux comme il arrive quelquefois pour la mer, elle semblait éprouver une tristesse d'exilée. *D'autres jours*, sa figure plus lisse engluait les désirs à sa surface vernie et les empêchait d'aller au delà; *à moins que* je ne la visse tout à coup de côté, car ses joues mates comme une blanche cire à la surface étaient roses par transparence, ce qui donnait tellement envie de les embrasser, d'atteindre ce teint différent qui se dérobait. *D'autres fois*, le bonheur baignait ces joues d'une clarté si mobile que la peau, devenue fluide et vague, laissait passer comme des regards sous-jacents qui la faisaient paraître d'une autre couleur, mais non d'une autre matière, que les yeux; *quelquefois*, sans y penser, quand on regardait sa figure ponctuée de petits points bruns et où flottaient seulement deux taches plus bleues; C'était comme on eût fait d'un oeuf de chardonneret, *souvent* comme d'une agate opaline travaillée et polie à deux places seulement où, au milieu de la pierre brune, luisaient, comme les ailes transparentes d'un papillon d'azur, les yeux où la chair devient miroir et nous donne l'illusion de nous laisser, plus qu'en les autres parties du corps, approcher de l'âme. Mais *le plus souvent* aussi elle était plus colorée, et alors plus animée: *quelquefois* seul était rose, dans sa figure blanche, le bout de son nez, fin comme celui d'une petite chatte sournoise avec qui l'on aurait eu envie de jouer; *quelquefois* ses joues étaient si lisses que le regard glissait comme sur celui d'une miniature sur leur émail rose, que faisait encore paraître plus delicat, plus intérieur, le couvercle entr'ouvert et superposé de ses cheveux noirs; *il arrivait que* le teint de ses joues atteingnît le rose violacé du cyclamen, et *parfois* même, quand elle était congestionnée ou fiévreuse, et donnant alors l'idée d'une complexion

maladive qui rabaissait mon désir à quelque chose de plus sen-
suel et faisait exprimer à son regard quelque chose de plus per-
vers et de plus malsain, la sombre pourpre de certaines roses
d'un rouge presque noir; et chacune de ces Albertine était
différente, comme est différente chacune des apparitions de la
danseuse dont sont transmutées les couleurs, la forme, le car-
actère, selon les jeux innombrablement variés d'un projecteur lu-
mineux. (Italics added.) [1]

On certain days, slim, with grey cheeks, a sullen air, a violet
transparency falling obliquely from her such as we notice
sometimes on the sea, she seemed to be feeling the sorrows of
exile. *On other days* her face, more sleek, caught and glued my
desires to its varnished surface and prevented them from going
any farther; *unless* I caught a sudden glimpse of her from the
side, for her dull cheeks, like white wax on the surface, were
visibly pink beneath, which made me anxious to kiss them, to
reach that different tint, which thus avoided my touch. *At
other times* happiness bathed her cheeks with a clarity so mobile that the skin, grown fluid and vague, gave passage to a
sort of stealthy and sub-cutaneous gaze, which made it appear
to be of another colour but not of another substance than her
eyes; *sometimes*, instinctively, when one looked at her face
punctuated with tiny brown marks among which floated what
were simply two larger, bluer stains, it was like looking at the
egg of a goldfinch—or *often* like an opalescent agate cut and
polished in two places only, where, from the heart of the
brown stone, shone like the transparent wings of a sky-blue
butterfly her eyes, those features in which the flesh becomes a
mirror and gives us the illusion that it allows us, more than

[1] All citations are from the Pléiade edition of *A la recherche du
temps perdu*. The English version of this passage and of the passage on page 112 is from the translation by C. K. Scott Moncrieff,
published by Random House. Translations in the text are by Paul
De Man.

through the other parts of the body, to approach the soul. But *most often of all* she shewed more colour, and was then more animated; *sometimes* the only pink thing in her white face was the tip of her nose, as finely pointed as that of a mischievous kitten with which one would have liked to stop and play; *sometimes* her cheeks were so glossy that one's glance slipped, as over the surface of a miniature, over their pink enamel, which was made to appear still more delicate, more private, by the enclosing though half-opened case of her black hair; *or it might happen that* the tint of her cheeks had deepened to the violet shade of the red cyclamen, and, *at times, even*, when she was flushed or feverish, with a suggestion of unhealthiness which lowered my desire to something more sensual and made her glance expressive of something more perverse and un-wholesome, to the deep purple of certain roses, a red that was almost black; and each of these Albertines was different, as in every fresh appearance of the dancer whose colours, form, character, are transmuted according to the innumerably varied play of a projected limelight (I, 708; italics added).

The two devices (internal delimitation and internal specifi-cation) can be used together in the same passage, as in this scene from *Combray* that deals in a general way with returns from walks. The general statement is then diversified by a de-limitation (itself iterative, since it recurs every year) that dis-tinguishes between the beginning and the end of the season. This second sequence is then again diversified by a single in-definite specification: "certains soirs. . . ." The following pas-sage is built on such a system; very simple but very produc-tive:

Nous rentrions *toujours* de bonne heure de nos promenades, pour pouvoir faire une visite à ma tante Léonie avant le dîner. *Au commencement de la saison*, où le jour finit tôt, quand nous arrivions rue du Saint-Esprit, il y avait encore un reflet du couchant sur les vitres de la maison et un bandeau de pourpre au fond des bois du Calvaire, qui se reflétait plus loin dans l'étang, rougeur qui, accompagnée souvent d'un froid assez vif, s'associait, dans mon esprit, à la rougeur du feu au-dessus duquel rôtissait le poulet qui ferait succéder pour moi au plaisir poétique donné par la promenade, le plaisir de la gourmandise, de la chaleur et du repos. *Dans l'été, au contraire,* quand nous rentrions le soleil ne se couchait pas encore; et pendant la visite que nous faisions chez ma tante Léonie, sa lumière qui s'abaissait et touchait la fenêtre, était arrêtée entre les grands rideaux et les embrasses, divisée, ramifiée, filtrée, et, incrustant de petits morceaux d'or le bois de citronnier de la commode, illuminait obliquement la chambre avec la délica-tesse qu'elle prend dans les sous-bois. Mais, *certains jours forts rares,* quand nous rentrions, il y avait bien longtemps que la commode avait perdu ses incrustations momentanées, il n'y avait plus, quand nous arrivions rue du Saint-Esprit, nul reflet de couchant étendu sur les vitres, et l'étang au pied du calvaire avait perdu sa rougeur, quelquefois il était déjà couleur d'opale, et un long rayon de lune, qui allait en s'élargissant et se fendillait de toutes les rides de l'eau, le traversait tout entier. (I, 133; italics added.)

We used *always* to return from our walks in good time to pay aunt Léonie a visit before dinner. *In the first weeks of our Combray holidays,* when the days ended early, we would still be able to see, as we turned into the Rue du Saint-Esprit, a re-flection of the western sky from the windows of the house and a band of purple at the foot of the Calvary, which was mir-rored further on in the pond; a fiery glow which, accompa-nied often by a cold that burned and stung, would associate itself in my mind with the glow of the fire over which, at that very moment, was roasting the chicken that was to furnish me, in place of the poetic pleasure I had found in my walk, with the sensual pleasures of good feeding, warmth and rest. *But in summer*, when we came back to the house, the sun would not have set; and while we were upstairs paying our visit to aunt Léonie its rays, sinking until they touched and lay along her window-sill, would there be caught and held by the large inner curtains and the bands which tied them back to the wall, and split and scattered and filtered; and then, at last, would fall upon and inlay with tiny flakes of gold the lemonwood of her chest-of-drawers, illuminating the room in their passage with the same delicate, slanting, shadowed beams that fall among the boles of forest trees. *But on some days, though very rarely,* the chest-of-drawers would long since have shed its momentary adornments, there would no longer, as we turned into the Rue du Saint-Esprit, be any reflection from the western sky burning along the line of window-panes; the pond beneath the Calvary would have lost its fiery glow, sometimes indeed had changed already to an opalescent pallor, while a long ribbon of moonlight, bent and broken and broadened by every ripple upon the water's surface, would be lying across it, from end to end (I, 102; italics added).

Finally, when all the resources of iterative particularization have been exhausted, two devices remain. I have already mentioned pseudo-iteration (as in the conversations between Françoise and Aunt Léonie); this is admittedly a way of cheating or, at the very least, of stretching the reader's benevolence to the limit. The second device is more honest—if such ethical terminology can have any sense in the world of art—but it represents an extreme case leading out of the actually iterative mode: in the midst of an iterative section the narrator mentions a particular, singular occurrence, either as illustration, or example, or, on the contrary, as an exception to the law of repetition that has just been established. Such moments can be introduced by an expression such as "thus it happened that . . ." ("c'est ainsi que . . .") or, in the case of an excep-

tion, "this time however . . ." ("une fois pourtant . . ."). The
following passage from the *Jeunes filles* is an example of the
first possibility: "*At times*, a kind gesture of one [of the girls]
would awaken within me an expansive sympathy that re-
placed, for a while, my desire for the others. *Thus it happened
that* Albertine, one day . . ." etc. (I, 911).[2] The famous passage of the Martinville clock towers is an example of the second possibility. It is explicitly introduced as an exception to
the habitual pattern: generally, when Marcel returns from
walks, he forgets his impressions and does not try to interpret
their meaning. "This time, however" (the expression is in
the text), he goes further and composes the descriptive piece
that constitutes his first literary work. The exceptional nature
of an event is perhaps even more explicitly stressed in a passage from *La Prisonnière* that begins as follows: "*I will put
aside*, among the days during which I lingered at Mme de
Guermantes's, one day that was marked by a small incident . . . ," after which the iterative narrative resumes: "*Except for this single incident*, everything went *as usual* when
I returned from the Duchess's . . ." (III, 54 and 55).[3]

By means of such devices, the singulative mode merges, so to
speak, with the iterative section and is made to serve it by positive or negative illustrations, either by adhering to the code or
by transgressing it—which is another way of recognizing its
existence.

The final problem associated with iterative temporality con-

[2] "*Parfois* une gentille attention de telle ou telle éveillait en moi
d'amples vibrations qui éloignaient pour un temps le désir des
autres. *Ainsi un jour* Albertine . . ."

[3] "*Je mettrai à part*, parmi ces jours où je m'attardai chez Mme de
Guermantes, un qui fut marqué par un petit incident . . ."; "*Sauf
cet incident unique*, tout se passait *normalement* quand je remon-
tais de chez la duchesse . . ."

cerns the relationship between the duration or, rather, the internal diachrony of the iterative unit under consideration, and the external diachrony, that is, the flow of "real" and necessarily singulative time between the beginning and the end of the iterative sequence. A unit such as "sleepless night," made up of a sequence that stretches over several years, may very well be told in terms of its own duration from night to morning, without reference to the external passage of years. The typical night remains constant, except for internal specifications, from the beginning to the end of the sequence, without being influenced by the passage of time outside the particular iterative unit. This is, in fact, what happens in the first pages of the *Recherche*. However, by means of internal delimitations, the narrative of an iterative unit may just as readily encompass the external diachrony and narrate, for example, "a Sunday at Combray" by drawing attention to changes in the dominical ritual brought about by the passage of years: greater maturity of the protagonist, new acquaintances, new interests, etc. In the Combray episodes, Proust very skillfully plays upon these possibilities. J. P. Houston claimed that the narrative progresses simultaneously on three levels: with the duration of the day, of the season, and of the years. Things are perhaps not quite as clear and systematic as Houston makes them out to be, but it is true that, in the Sunday scenes, events taking place in the afternoon are of a later date than those taking place in the morning and that, in the narration of the walks, the most recent episodes are assigned to the longest itineraries. For the reader, this creates the illusion of a double temporal progression, as if the hero were a naïve little boy in the morning and a sophisticated adolescent at night, aging several years in the course of a single day or a single walk. We are touching here upon the outer limits of the iterative narrative mode.

Thus Proust appears to substitute for the *summary*, which typifies the classical novel, another form of synthesis, the iterative narrative. The synthesis is no longer achieved by acceleration, but by analogy and abstraction. The rhythm of Proust's narrative is no longer founded, as in the classical *récit*, on the alternating movement of dramatic and summarizing sections, but on the alternating movement of iterative and singular scenes. Most of the time, these alternating sections overlay a system of hierarchical subordinations that can be revealed by analysis. We already encountered two types of such systems: an iterative-explanatory section that is functionally dependent on an autonomous singular episode: the Guermantes wit (iterative) in the midst of a dinner at the duchess's (singular): and a singular-illustrative section dependent on an autonomous iterative sequence (in the scenes used as illustrations or exceptions). The hierarchical systems of interdependence can be more complex, as when a singular scene illustrates an iterative section that is itself inserted within another singulative scene: this happens, for example, when a particular anecdote (such as Oriane's wordplay on Taquin le Superbe) is used to illustrate the famous Guermantes wit: here we have a singulative element (Taquin le Superbe) within an iterative sequence (Guermantes wit) itself included in a singulative scene (dinner at Oriane de Guermantes's). The description of these structural relationships is one of the tasks of narrative analysis.

It often happens that the relationships are less clear and that the Proustian narrative fluctuates between the two modes without visible concern for their respective functions, without even seeming to be aware of the differences. Some time ago, Marcel Vigneron pointed out confusions of this sort in the section dealing with Marcel's love for Gilberte at the Champs-Elysées: an episode would start off in the historical past (*passé défini*), continue in the imperfect, and return to the historical past, without any possibility for the reader to determine whether he was reading a singular or an iterative scene. Vigneron attributed these anomalies to last-minute changes in the manuscript made necessary by publication. The explanation may be correct, but it is not exhaustive, for similar discrepancies occur at other moments in the *Recherche* when no such considerations of expediency can be invoked. Proust probably at times forgets what type of narrative he is using; hence, for example, the very revealing sudden appearance of a historical past within a pseudo-iterative scene (I, 104, 722). He was certainly also guided by a secret wish to set the narrative forms free from their hierarchical function, letting them play and "make music" for themselves, as Proust himself said of Flaubert's ellipses. Hence the most subtle and admirable passages of all, of which J. P. Houston has mentioned a few, in which Proust passes from an iterative to a singular passage or uses an almost imperceptible modulation—such as an ambiguous imperfect of which it is impossible to know whether it functions iteratively or singularly, or the interposition of directly reported dialogue without declarative verb and, consequently, without determined mode, or a page of commentary by the narrator, in the present tense—to achieve the opposite effect; such a modulation, lengthily developed and to all appearances carefully controlled, serves as a transition between the first eighty pages of *La Prisonnière* that are in an iterative mode, and the singulative scenes that follow.

I have particularly stressed the question of narrative frequency because it has often been neglected by critics and by theoreticians of narrative technique, and because it occupies a particularly prominent place in the work of Marcel Proust. A paper that deals so sketchily and provisionally with a single category of narrative discourse cannot hope to reach a conclusion. Let me therefore end by pointing out that, together with the daring manipulations of chronology I have mentioned in the first part of my paper and the large-sized distortions of duration described in the second, Proust's predilection for an iterative narrative mode and the complex and subtle manner in which he exploits the contrasts and relations of this mode with a singulative discourse combine to free his narrative forever from the constraints and limitations of traditional narration. For it goes without saying that, in an iterative temporality, the order of succession and the relationships of duration that make up classical temporality are from the very beginning subverted or, more subtly and effectively, *perverted*. Proust's novel is not only what it claims to be, a novel of time lost and recaptured, but also, perhaps more implicitly, a novel of controlled, imprisoned, and bewitched time, a part of what Proust called, with reference to dreams, "the formidable game it plays with Time" ("le jeu formidable qu'il fait avec le Temps").

(Translated by Paul De Man)

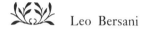 Leo Bersani

PROUST AND THE ART
OF INCOMPLETION

For Flaubert, the success of art depends on its ability to provide a definitive image of a reality anterior to art. Although the end of *Madame Bovary* gives to the novel a dimension it cannot explore but merely points to—that of a social order best characterized by the place it allows for the apothecary, M. Homais—this open-endedness is more apparent than real within the structure of the work. In its references to social history, *Madame Bovary* is deliberately incomplete, but formally its ending authentically concludes the work by helping, like the beginning, to enclose Emma's life within a larger and less analytically detailed picture of French provincial life. The intended finality of the work is indirectly reflected in Flaubert's awkward transitions from paragraph to paragraph and from chapter to chapter. His notion of style imprisons him in isolated, drawn-out battles with each narrative unit. And between the perfect and perfectly self-contained sentences and paragraphs, there is—ideally, we might also say—nothing but the creative void in which the novelist's work (his novel and his struggle) has simply ceased to exist.

When Proust's narrator praises, in *La Prisonnière*, the "marvelously incomplete" nature of nineteenth-century masterpieces, he is suggesting—hesitantly and ambivalently, it is true—that the most interesting fact about artistic creation may be the very *im*possibility of writing definitive sentences and definitive works. The passage I am thinking of (in which Marcel refers to Wagner, Hugo, Michelet, and Balzac) has several shifts of tone and position, for two very different things appeal to the Proustian narrator: the fragmentary nature of major artistic productions in the nineteenth century, and the notion that great art, by definition, has a "vital" unity and completeness which critical recognition can make explicit but does not create. I think that the latter expresses a nostalgic view of the relation of art to the world and to the self which the narrator's experience tends most profoundly to undermine. And we can easily see the possibly radical consequences of Marcel's admiration for what he calls the "literary miscarriages" of the nineteenth century's "greatest writers." If the quality of completeness is recognized as a cultural imperative rather than an attribute inherent to art, art runs the risk of losing the privileged status it has always been granted among life's activities. If, like other processes in life, it can never be thought of as "completed," it no longer stands as a kind of epistemological monument in relation to the rest of our experience. Art ceases to reassure us about reality as intrinsically meaningful and conclusively shaped. The real is no longer the *object* of art any more than it is the object of any other activity—like making love or playing chess—which simply coexists with all the other activities we call reality. It then naturally becomes much more difficult than ever before to de-

fine what is specifically "artistic" about the activity of art, and
the attempt to do so has, in the modern period, given us works
which have become more and more open-ended and purely in-
terrogative. Is art *about* anything? Is there a subject "behind"
the work? Do we have to discard an aesthetic of imitation or
expressiveness?

At the extreme limit of this problematic self-reflection in
contemporary literature, we have, in Maurice Blanchot and in
Samuel Beckett, a literature about the necessity of its own failure. The narrator of *A la recherche du temps perdu* is, of
course, far from maintaining that the most interesting nineteenth-century artists are great *because* they failed. But his remarks in *La Prisonnière* correspond to the most original aspects of his own literary achievement. It is the lifelike
incompleteness of that achievement which I want to examine.
The Proustian art of incompletion has helped to subvert an
aesthetic of art as the lifeless if instructive museum where we
enter, in the "pauses" of experience, to replenish ourselves with
the dead significance of safely immutable trophies of life.

The correspondences which Proust's narrator will establish
between art and the rest of his life appear to have, as their
point of departure, questions raised by Flaubert in order to assert the separation between art and life. A Flaubertian preoccupation with the correspondences between language and reality would seem also to characterize Marcel in *A la recherche
du temps perdu*. But the problem is posed in a way which
brings Proust's work, in spite of its bleak analyses of human
possibilities, closer to the most optimistic Stendhalian assertions
of human freedom than to the nihilistic conclusions of *Madame Bovary* and *L'education sentimentale*. For Flaubert, the
experience of dealing novelistically with the question of how
expressive words are of reality does nothing to change the way

in which he asks the question. Emma's tragedy is the result of what we might call her uncritical dependence on Flaubert's formulation of the novelistic dilemma. Apparently, nothing that happened in the writing of *Madame Bovary* led Flaubert to suspect that he had perhaps created an unnecessary dead-end in thinking that art must be a perfect fit between expression and a preexistent reality. And Emma does nothing but reenact the same assumptions from, as it were, the other direction. Flaubert dreams of a style adequate to the independent reality of his subjects; Emma searches for the reality adequate to the vocabulary of romantic clichés.

Because Flaubert immediately equates having experience with a problem of verbal designation, language blocks Flaubert's interest in discriminating among the choices by which we experiment with different ways of defining the self and the world. The very fact that language has to be used in making such choices leads Flaubert to a tortured weighing of the instruments available to describe them. He is indifferent to the commitments which a *use* of language creates, and because he thus isolates language from the activities it inspires and accompanies, words naturally appear to have a frighteningly impersonal life of their own. In one sense, Flaubert's disgust with life could be explained by his never having *reached* life in his epistemological investigations. And his choice of art as an alternative to life is, as the progress of his fiction from *Madame Bovary to Bouvard et Pécuchet* suggests, just as much a rejection of art as it is of life. His activity in both is paralyzed by his reluctance to examine the consequences of different uses of language and his obsession with its supposed essence.

Superficially, Proust's narrator is as concerned as Flaubert and Emma with the problem of what words designate. Marcel's life, like Emma's, appears to be structured by a series of hopeful fantasies and "falls": Mme de Guermantes does not provide the reality needed to make the notion of Merovingian mysteries come alive, Balbec does not embody the idea of nature's glamorously violent life, and Berma's acting, at first, cannot be fitted to the notion of dramatic talent. During his adolescence, Marcel, a little like Emma, waits for life to bring what he vaguely but passionately expects from it. Fascinated by words—the names of people and of places, and moral abstractions—he strains anxiously to receive "the secret of Truth and Beauty, things half-felt by me, half-incomprehensible, the full understanding of which was the vague but permanent object of my thoughts." The disappointments Marcel suffers are of course important, but, interestingly enough, they do not provoke an obsessive mistrust of thought and language. And this, I think, is because his sense of self is so dependent on the shape of his expectations that their destruction literally *empties* his imagination. As a result, the Flaubertian rhythm of illusion and disillusion is redefined by Proust as a discordance between the self and the world rather than as an imbalance between inexhaustible, impersonal fictions and a reality which is always either hypothetical and beyond language (Flaubert's Platonic subject) or flatly material and inferior to language (Tostes and Yonville).

The fragility of Marcel's sense of self will of course be recognized by readers of Proust as the principal "theme" of Marcel's life. It is the source of an anguish from which there seemed no escape at Combray and which only literature can provide a way of circumventing or, more exactly, of transforming into a creative exhilaration. *A la recherche* is punctuated by crucial episodes which dramatize a spectacular loss of being: the description at the beginning of *Combray* of the narrator's dizzying flights from one bedroom to another—

and from one identity to another—when he awakes at night not knowing where, and therefore who, he is; the child's panic when he is separated from his mother at night; Marcel's horror at being surrounded, in the Balbec hotel room, by "enemies," by "things which did not know me"; and the emptiness of personality ("I was nothing more than a heart that throbbed") which prevents Marcel from recognizing the city of Venice when his mother angrily leaves without him for the railway station. In none of these cases is it a question of the Flaubertian excess of designation which removes the individual from the world and imprisons him in a rich but objectless imagination. Rather, the failure to recognize a place is experienced as a failure of all designation—most painfully, as a failure of self-recognition.

Such incidents could, I think, be traced to Marcel's sense of the sinfully individualizing nature of desire. Marcel's desires —sexual, social, and aesthetic—define his self; they express his designs on the world and give to his history its personal shape. But he feels a guilt about individuality which seems to be passed from his mother to Marcel: she herself attempts to erase all signs of her own personality after her mother's death, for anything purely self-expressive might be a blasphemous violation of Marcel's grandmother's memory. It is as if Marcel came to feel that *any* desires directed somewhere else (the loved one's sexual interest in someone else is the most dramatic version of this) express a sinister project for independence. They threaten the fantasy of a tranquil, really deathlike coincidence of being between two people in which each one merely receives, is wholly contained within, and sends back the image of the other. This is the security Marcel yearns for between himself and his mother and grandmother, and the two women seem to encourage this cult of love as self-sacrificial and yet all-devouring. To desire a peasant girl from Méséglise or the baronne de Putbus's chambermaid is to be someone different from *maman;* thus desire is felt—with guilt—as dangerously aggressive because Marcel knows that in fact it is an aggression against those who would fix and limit his own being in their love. To immolate desire is to immolate the self; it is the payment he has to make in order not to escape from his mother's attention, in order to continue "receiving himself" from her.

And yet the temptation to be—which is the temptation of freedom—is painfully strong. Because Marcel seems to condemn his own passionate projects and desires as a betrayal of his mother, and because the resulting conflict over them increases their potency while limiting their frequency of expression, he comes to fear them, without, however, renouncing the independent identity they create. If the loss of self is the punishment for desire—that is, for energetic designs on the world—some new form of self-assertion becomes necessary in order to protect Marcel from the consequences of self-assertion. The very extremity to which he is reduced—his emptiness, his loss of memory, the discontinuity of being from which he suffers—authorizes the most thoroughgoing investigation of ways to construct and possess a self which could no longer be lost. The punishment, we might say, legitimizes the crime. Literature in *A la recherche du temps perdu* is Marcel's indulgence in the "crime" of his own individuality as well as his subtle strategy for imprisoning others within the designs of his own desires. But in the enactment of what can easily be seen in Proust as an ungenerous solution to this problem of being, the project of imprisoning the self and the world in a document of ontological security is transformed into the courageous exercise of making the self as indefinite and indefinable as possible, and even of protecting the freedom of others.

We can easily see the continuity between the drastic self-depletions from which Marcel suffers and the narrator's ambivalent attitude toward "incomplete" art. The dream of art as a way of achieving a deathlike fixity of self in life, for example, has the appeal of promising a kind of sculptural organization of the self and the world into immutably intelligible patterns. To salvage the self from the dissipation it suffers at moments of passionate desire, Marcel, while he never really considers the renunciation of desire, is tempted by the possibility of satisfying desires by de-energizing them. A certain self-petrification would seem to be the compromise between an uninhibited appetitive attack on the world and the probably expiatory victimizing of a "throbbing heart" by a world hostilely different from the self. And the perspective of memory allows for just this sort of passionless reenactment of desires, although, as we shall presently see, it also can permit a manipulating of the past for the sake of a richer future. In part, Proust's novel illustrates the truth of Sartre's claim that only in reflection can we posit affectivity for itself, that is, in terms of mental *states* which make for a psychology of the inert. Cut off from the objects which inspired and defined them, Marcel's desires, so to speak, no longer have anywhere to go. They do not "move" toward the world, but only around one another, creating those peculiar inner constellations which encourage the narrator to speak of mental life as if it were organized into clearly delimited conflicting states, and enacted as allegorical confrontations. Thus the narrator can at last live according to his desires, or, more exactly, *within* his desires. The retrospective expression of desire coincides with self-possession. Indeed, it belatedly constructs a self shaped by projects now transformed into abstractions. The psychology of states in *A la recherche du temps perdu*, like the general laws about human behavior, allows Marcel to think of literature as the reassuring completion of life. Both are maneuvers for placing art in the privileged position of giving permanent forms and significance to experience; as the place in which psychological truths are distilled, the narrator's work defines and closes his life.

But Marcel discovers another possibility of self-identification (as well as of contact with the world), a possibility which allows for a richly incomplete life and a richly incomplete work. Marcel's jealousy can provide a first illustration of how this discovery is made. In *La Fugitive*, the narrator speaks of a certain "compensation" in the suffering which the lies of "insensitive and inferior women" inflict on sensitive and intellectual men. Behind each of the loved one's words, the narrator writes, such men "feel that a lie is lurking, behind each house to which she says that she has gone, another house, behind each action, each person, another action, another person." And, he concludes, "all this creates, in front of the sensitive and intelligent man, a universe [in depths] which his jealousy would fain plumb and which is not without interest to his intelligence." Any statement felt or recognized as a lie evokes the possibly truthful statements to which it could be compared. But if the lover cannot fix on any one house or action or person as the reality behind the lie, the lie itself can never be eliminated from the attempt to know the truth. The fictive version of their behavior proposed by Albertine or Odette becomes the center on which Marcel and Swann organize a group of conjectures. The pain of not being able to eliminate that center—it is necessary to inspire the different conjectures whose lesser or greater probability it also helps to determine—is somewhat compensated for by the variety and depth which the lover's searching and unsatisfied imagination gives to the world. The need for truth stimulates the novelistic impulse, and the impossibility of truth makes of experience an infinitely expandable novel.

Involuntary memories provide a similar variety of points of view, and this time we can see more explicitly how expandable versions of experience in *A la recherche* are equivalent to expansive self-definitions. Numerous commentators have rightly emphasized the importance of involuntary memories in the novel, but it seems to me that the crucial role they play in Proust's work derives from what most of his readers have been unwilling to admit: their extremely modest significance. Involuntary memory is a brief coincidence between a present moment and a past one: a sensation now (such as the taste of the *madeleine*) accidentally awakens the full sensory memory of a past experience, and, "for the duration of a lightning flash," Marcel appears to exist "between" the present and the past, that is, in the similarity between the two—a similarity which is actually an abstraction from experience but which the senses fleetingly live. Now these memories *create* nothing; the extra-temporal essence which the narrator claims they disengage from a present sensation and a past sensation may not have been previously felt as such, but it is nonetheless a truth about Marcel's *history* of sensations and in itself it contains nothing to inspire a future.

The interest of the so-called essences which involuntary memories reveal is that they make impossible any definitive self-formulations. The towel with which Marcel wipes his mouth in the Guermantes library, having "precisely the same sort of starchy stiffness as the towel with which I had so much trouble drying myself before the window the first day of my stay at Balbec," evokes a vision of "azure blue," spreads out, "in its various folds and creases, like a peacock's tail, the plumage of a green and blue ocean. And I drew enjoyment, not only from those colours, but from a whole moment of my life which had brought them into being and had no doubt been an aspiration toward them, but which perhaps some feeling of fatigue or sadness had prevented me from enjoying at Balbec and which now, pure and disembodied, freed from all the imperfections of objective perception, filled me with joy." This remark from *Le Temps retrouvé* implies nothing less than a reorganization of the hierarchy of interests and projects by which we rationally, and most habitually, recognize and define ourselves. It would be banal merely to point out that we are never completely aware of all our interests in any given situation. But, first of all, involuntary memory is a particularly powerful proof of this. Furthermore, Marcel's "return" to Balbec in the Guermantes library undermines the anxiety he felt at the time. It suggests that at least as strong as his fears was an aspiration toward certain colors, a thirst for sensations which complicates the episode of his arrival at Balbec by making it impossible for us—and for him—to settle on any one characterization of his feelings. Involuntary memory, while it appears to offer evidence of "an individual, identical and permanent self," and thus appeases Marcel's fear of psychological discontinuity, also *dislocates* self-definitions by illustrating how incomplete they always are.

The importance of this is somewhat obscured by the narrator's emphatic distinctions between loss of self and self-possession; but the strategies for self-possession are by no means strategies for permanent self-immobilizations. And involuntary memory "returns" Marcel to himself at the same time that it demolishes the coherent views of his past which, in spite of the crises in which he seems to lose his past, he of course possesses all the time in his intellectual or voluntary memory. The taste of the *madeleine* and the sensations in the Guermantes library are trivial and tentative self-possessions, and this is exactly why they point the way to a literature of inventive autobiography. The essence liberated by an involuntary memory is, therefore, first of all personal: it is not in things, but in the particular analogies or identities which Marcel's sensory apparatus establishes among sensations. And it is in no sense the essence of his personality; it is, instead, just the essence of a particular relation in his history. Finally, by relocating or at least raising doubts about what was most important to him at a past moment, Marcel's involuntary memories legitimize an open-ended view of personality which informs the psychologically re-creative activity of writing *A la recherche du temps perdu*.

"Informs" in what way, exactly? How is the view of the self which I find implicit in Marcel's involuntary memories expressed and confirmed by style and novelistic structure in *A la recherche*? If what the narrator calls the "fundamental notes" of personality is inadequately rendered in the language we ordinarily use in our attempts to be recognized by others as belonging to a life already familiar to them, he must find a language which contains his most personal accent without, however, sacrificing the signs by which that accent may be communicated to others. The solution to this problem depends on the literary exploitation of what we might call experimental knowledge through self-disguises. Now the disguises of personality have both a positive and a negative value in *A la recherche*. The narrator insists so often on the pain caused by such disguises that we may not see at once the extent of his own indulgence in a liberating art of disguise. Sexuality—

especially homosexuality—is presented in the novel as the field in which the Proustian "creatures of flight" can most effectively conceal their personalities by "dressing" them in desires inconceivable to the pursuing and possessive lover. Marcel cannot understand the "play" of Albertine's Lesbianism because he cannot imagine what "role" she plays in it. Her love of women is an impenetrable disguise of his own love of women; she has his desires, but since she is a woman, he cannot recognize himself in them.

The connection between complicated sexual roles and the willful elusiveness of personality is most strikingly dramatized in the scene at Rachel's theater in *Le Côté de Guermantes*. Rachel's flirtation with a young male dancer who reminds her of another woman and to whom she speaks of having "a wonderful time" with him "and a girl I know" plunges Saint-Loup's jealous imagination into a labyrinth of psychological disguises. Images of desire become inextricably embroiled in a costume play in which the man would presumably be playing the role of a woman for Rachel or her friend, or for both, and they might be taking the role of a man with a man looking like a woman. Finally, the most baroque costumes of sexual desire are evoked in the letter Charlus accidentally reads from the Lesbian actress Léa to Morel. In it Léa uses an expression about Morel which Charlus has always associated with homosexuality ("Toi tu en es au moins"), but homosexuality here seems to mean that Morel has "the same taste as certain women for other women." Poor Charlus finds himself confronted with "the sudden inadequacy of a definition," and the letter sets up an unsolvable problem for the baron's imagination: by what images and identifications can the homosexual man calm his jealousy of another homosexual man who finds his pleasure with Lesbians? "Where" is Morel in such pleasures? What is it like to be a man being treated like a woman who desires women acting like men?

Such are the disguises of escape from others, disguises which, as we see in Rachel's case, can be sadistically adopted in order to make the lover suffer from a spectacularly mysterious assertion of otherness. But in the literary work which devotes so much space to the anguished documentation of this sinister art of self-concealment, the narrator discovers other techniques of self-diffusion, techniques which transform the accidental and infrequent "airing" of personality which involuntary memories provide into a willed and continuous process of self-renewal. I am thinking mainly of the therapeutical diffusiveness of metaphorical representation in art. Analogy in *A la recherche* is often humorous. This is especially evident when the narrator compares some prosaic aspect of his past to an illustrious historical event. Françoise's passionate and fearful commentary of Léonie's slightest change of mood, of the way she gets up in the morning or has a meal, reminds the narrator of the nobility's anxious attentiveness to almost imperceptible signs of favor or disfavor in Louis XIV. And the cruelty with which Françoise strangles the chickens she serves to Marcel's family at Combray changes the boy's view of her moral merits and makes him think of all the brutality hidden behind the official piety with which royal figures from the past are represented to us in religious art. Finally, the water lily ceaselessly carried from one bank of the Vivonne to the other by the river's currents fascinates Marcel, who watches it thinking of the "strange, ineluctable, fatal daily round" in the habits of "certain victims of neurasthenia," and then expands his analogy to include an illustrious literary precedent which, by a final humorous twist, brings him back to his own staring at the "possessed" plant: "Such as these [the victims of neurasthenia] was the water-lily, and also like one of those wretches whose peculiar torments, repeated indefinitely throughout eternity, aroused the curiosity of Dante, who would have inquired of them at greater length and in fuller detail from the victims themselves, had not Virgil, striding on ahead, obliged him to hasten after him at full speed, as I must hasten after my parents."

On the one hand, such analogies make fun of Françoise, Léonie, and Marcel; they give a mock-heroic importance to the most unremarkable events or habits in their lives. But they also trivialize life at Versailles and Dante's trip through hell. From both points of view, the uniqueness of each element in the metaphor is undermined by its availability for an unexpected comparison. The analogies clarify, but they are also reductive, and they easily serve intentions of mockery. Historical repetition may be instructive, but it also parodies individuality; or, perhaps more precisely, it makes us skeptical about or indifferent to individuality since the quality which two incidents have in common is detached from the historical existence of each incident. Life at Versailles is an episodic illustration of a *type* of life reincarnated in a scene from French provincial life at the end of the nineteenth century. Now such historical continuities are exactly what the narrator finds, or invents, as he writes the story of his own life. But the repetitions of autobiography are of course *self*-repetitions. And in the purely verbal organization of a literary work, the chronological sequence of events can be thought of as spatialized in constellations of literary metaphors. From his perspective of re-creative memories, the narrator constantly anticipates future events by "trying them out" metaphorically before they happen. Georges Poulet has spoken of a "reciprocal intelligibility" among originally distinct episodes in Marcel's life; analogies establish patterns that bring together apparently isolated moments, and they both evoke what has already been written and point to what is yet to be written.

This network of metaphorical correspondences does give to the work what at first appears to be a self-contained unity. But, more originally, such correspondences are also psychologically disintegrating. They have the effect of drawing us away from any fixed *center* of the self from which all its images might proceed. It has often been said that the narrator has very little personality compared to the other characters of *A la recherche*. And this is usually meant as an adverse judgment of the novel: as B. G. Rogers puts it, ". . . the absence of a real hero in Marcel is hard to reconcile with the massive emotional and spiritual emphasis placed upon him in *Le Temps Retrouvé*." This impression is particularly interesting in view of the fact that no reader can be unaware of the psychological repetitiveness in *A la recherche du temps perdu*. And the narrator does tell us enough about himself so that we easily recognize the psychological patterns repeated throughout the novel as belonging to *his* personality. It is nonetheless true that he tends to disappear as the visible and sharply defined source of those patterns. But I take this to be the sign of the narrator's most impressive achievement. The vagueness of Marcel as the center of his world can be the basis of a reproach only if we impose on the work notions of what it means "to have personality" which the work is engaged in discarding. What we might call the narrator's scattering of self is the technique of an often humorous and always liberating displacement of his most crippling fantasies. There is no one version of those fantasies more authoritative than other versions, and the self therefore has the freedom of *being* the variety of its disguises.

The various uses of metaphor in *A la recherche* have, fundamentally, the function of entertaining as many interpretive extensions of experience as possible. There is, for example, a certain type of social life which we recognize as the narrator's particular sense of society. And the continuities among different social images in the novel are often astonishingly transparent. The Verdurin receptions repeat details from the Guermantes receptions. La Patronne, like Oriane, boasts about the paintings Elstir did for her. An annoyance with illness and death because they spoil dinner parties and dances is repeated in progressively more shocking (and more improbable) versions: in the duc de Guermantes's refusal to be told that his cousin is dead at the end of *Le Côté de Guermantes;* in M. Verdurin's insisting, one day at la Raspelière, that no one speak of Dechambre's death to Mme Verdurin; and in the latter's nervy denial—during the party at the quai Conti in *La Prisonnière*—that she feels any sorrow over the princess Sherbatoff's death. We might say either that the narrator describes three different social events in a surprisingly similar manner, or that he finds impressively different disguises for a rather simple and bitter view of social life. But the various disguises of that view make it difficult to fix the exact quality of the pessimism. There is a greater tolerance of emotional callousness in the presentation of Oriane's inability to decide if she should give up her parties after Swann tells her he is going to die than in the image of Mme Verdurin's defiant advertising of her indifference to the princess's death. The second incident enacts a pessimistic view of social life in a manner more likely to shock the narrator out of social life. Each repetition of a radical skepticism about human feeling allows for different consequences, broadens or narrows the range of possible response to an essentially unchanged but nonetheless flexible conviction.

Furthermore, the world Marcel is presumably remembering strikes us in many respects as a projection of his own psychology and history. In the process of remembering an impenetrable world, and while documenting with somber lucidity the hopelessness of seeking to know the lives of others, Marcel has both illustrated his thesis and partially refuted it by now drawing the world of his past into the orbit of a single, recognizably continuous personality: his own. What might be called the creative space between the narrator and the world he describes—the actual work of self-dramatization which Balzac and Stendhal hide by suggesting that the decisions of writing are decisions of point of view toward a world already there—becomes a principal object of our attention in *A la recherche du temps perdu*. The novel provokes the drama of our own unsettled feelings about the exact sense in which these people and events belong to Marcel's past. And they seem to "belong" to *him* in an allegorical sense. The narrator thus seems to be illustrating, more or less transparently and in spite of his explicit claims that he is reporting on the real world of his past, the processes by which a novelist invents a world of fiction, and, more specifically, the degree of differentiation possible within a group of self-projective images.

Every incident and every character in *A la recherche* could be placed on a range of self-projection, a range extending from the most transparent versions of Marcel's psychology to those complexly particularized images in which allegory and observation appear to coincide. The inability to differentiate others from the self is dramatized within the novel as the anguish of love, at the same time that it defines the limits of characterization in a novel about love. Thus Albertine, by being so embroiled in Marcel's tortured doubts about her real personality, is an occasion for demonstrating an abortive attempt to disguise novelistic conjecture as a clear and fixed image of the external world. Saint-Loup and Mme de Guermantes, on the other hand, are so sharply individualized that they do seem to exist, so to speak, independently of the narrator's inventiveness, although Saint-Loup's love for Rachel parallels Marcel's possessively jealous love for Albertine, and Oriane's anxious reluctance (common to all the Guermantes) to let her guests leave at the end of a party reminds us of Marcel's terror at being separated from his mother. The psychology which we find so idiosyncratic and even pathological in *Combray* takes into account enough variety of experience so that its social "disguises" impress us as intelligent conclusions about life rather than the given limitations with which the narrator approaches life. If the world of Marcel's past becomes, in the process of writing, a fiction dramatizing Marcel himself, the very self-dramatization is such a liberal and inclusive one that it strikes us as a viable or livable framework in which to place the world.

Viable and therefore capable of development. What Marcel gives us is by no means a final, limiting version of experience. The fact that in describing the world he shapes it into an almost allegorical reflection of his own imagination diminishes the constraints of reality on his life. Superficially, this psychological repetitiousness in his work would seem to testify to the narrowness of his responses; more profoundly, by illustrating the power of his self-projections, it subverts the impoverishing authority of reality in whatever he says. No fact is strong enough to expel Marcel's fantasies from his report of it, which means that nothing in his life, short of death, can prevent him from using fact for a continuous revision of fantasy. He is as free as his imagination can make him precisely because, when he is most faithful to his experience, he has no illusion of being able to make statements about reality from which his imagination would be absent. The inconclusiveness of "knowledge" allows for the theoretically limitless use of the world as a testing-ground for fictions.

Flaubert's superstition of the real naturally led him to a process of constant deletion in his writing: how could he ever be sure that each sentence or each metaphor was not saying too much about reality, and therefore violating it? Proust, on the other hand, can add endlessly to his work, for it is as if he discovered, through his narrator's self-re-creative memory, that even the most oppressively narrow experience can be interpreted into a constantly open-ended view of the world. And there is nothing naïve in this. Objects and other people are present; they impinge on Marcel's consciousness and they make him suffer. But in the process of admitting his inability to possess and control them, he finds that the barrier of his subjectivity gives him another kind of power: the power to invent and revise the significance of events and, by the excesses of experimental revision, to coerce reality into the field of his desires.

We could even say that *because* everything that happens in *A la recherche* is in Marcel's past, he has never in his life enjoyed more freedom than now. The final, definitive quality of events is felt at the moment we live them. It is then that we experience most concretely the impoverishing limitations and exclusions implicit in each emotion we have, each spectacle we see, each decision we make. It is only in memory that the future of each moment appears promisingly uncertain and therefore open to possibility. For in memory we can profit from a larger notion of consequences than we can afford to use at the "first" or present version of each experience. Retrospectively, the immediate effects of events can be subverted by an interpretive will; at the actual time of those events, we were too busily engaged in their first consequences to see those consequences as anything but necessary and final. Proust's novel constantly illustrates this distinction; it is a literary dramatization of the psychoanalytic assumption that in certain conditions a restatement of the past creates new possibilities for the future. For all its apparent backward-looking, *A la recherche du temps perdu* is a more projective novel than, say, *La Chartreuse de Parme*. Fabrice only rushes forward in time, and the pathos of his life is that his experience creates an irreversible destiny. Life narrows the range of his projects until, with unattackable logic, he has nothing more to do but die. When he returns to his past it is to rest, not to re-create. Proust's narrator, in a characteristic gesture of false surrender, turns his back on life in order to make some extraordinary claims for the future of his life. Aggressively active and self-revising, he remakes a once disappointing past into the field of an extravagant exercise in self-expansion.

Repetition in *A la recherche* is therefore a mode of freedom. But while the freedom which the narrator enjoys throughout his work is self-creative, it also coincides with a kind of impersonality. His metaphorical style allows him to repeat himself at the same time that it raises the contents of self-definitions above any one embodiment of them. "In anyone we love," the narrator writes in *Le Temps retrouvé*, "there is always present some dream that we cannot always discern but which we constantly seek to attain. It was my faith in Bergotte and Swann which had made me love Gilberte, just as it was my belief in Gilbert the Bad which had made me love Mme. de Guermantes. And what a wide expanse of unfathomable ocean was set apart in my love for Albertine, painful, jealous and individual though that love was? Moreover, just on account of this individual quality which we pursue with such eagerness, our love for someone else is already somewhat of an aberration." Our loves are most deeply characterized by a "persistent, unconscious dream" which seeks to incarnate itself in various persons. The dream is a specific type of desire; *it expresses an individuality more general than individuals*. And that individuality is what Proust's narrator calls an "essence"; it belongs to "the world of differences" which only art reveals.

The individuality of a point of view embodied in but not dependent on the existence of an individual person: as Gilles Deleuze has brilliantly defined it, this is what the narrator comes to recognize as the source of the pleasure he experiences in front of great art. And this identification of the absolutely individual with a region of Being transcending individuals saves the Proustian narrator from the despair of feeling that language can never communicate the "fundamental notes" of an artist's personality. By distinguishing between individuality and what we ordinarily think of as subjectivity, he can entrust the expression of individuality to a system of communication in which meanings are always *shared* meanings. Only an aesthetic of the ineffably personal rejects words because of their inescapably generalizing nature. Nothing could be further from the kind of personality which *A la recherche du temps perdu* seeks to express. Its austere drama consists in the narrator's effort to *abstract* an individual style from a life in which style is constantly threatened by the obsessions of a particular existence.

The narrative texture of *A la recherche* is open-endedly metaphorical, which is one of the ways in which it differs most strikingly from that of *Jean Santeuil*. Metaphor in *Jean Santeuil* is essentially ornamental and psychologically distracting. In a sense, that novel is a far more "literary" or "written" work than *A la recherche*; it has an uninteresting stylistic complexity which makes each of its sections a self-contained, carefully wrought—overwrought—"piece." Proust could not, I think, have changed the essential discontinuity of *Jean Santeuil* by providing more links from one episode to another; to make smoother transitions would not have changed the underlying conception of style as an exercise of verbally enshrining disconnected experiences. As a result of this conception, incidents in *Jean Santeuil* often have a kind of depth which is largely eliminated from the later work. In *A la recherche*, on the one hand, metaphors enrich specific incidents without completely "covering" them; on the other hand, the freedom of the metaphors themselves is protected by their extensions into other parts of the novel, by their being containers always larger than whatever they contain at any given moment. There is no network of multiple interpretations in *Jean Santeuil*, and, consequently, we frequently *see through* episodes to a single, definite, and limiting significance. We may, for example, feel that Jean's overwhelmed reaction at the discovery that Charlotte is willing to give him certain erotic satisfactions is intelligible only if we think of the scene as a mask for an unexpected homosexual encounter. There is nothing in Proust's treatment of the scene which lifts it above the peculiarity of its literal detail. As far as "content" goes, *A la recherche* has equally peculiar episodes; but the style now has a centrifugal energy which prevents us from considering such content as the transparent sign of something unsaid, of a hidden reality. Incidents no longer extend "behind" themselves into the author's veiled psychology; instead, they are now coerced by metaphor into extensions leading to other metaphorical inventions throughout the novel. They are, as it were, horizontally rather than vertically transcendent. The significance of each passage is limited only by the amount of novelistic space which the narrator will have the time to fill in the process of self-enlargement which is his literary vocation.

Literature in Proust's world does involve a certain moving away from life. The image of the writer sealed up in his cork-lined room is a dramatic enough metaphor for that removal. But the narrator in his hermetic seclusion reveals the mechanisms of self-removal as operative throughout his life; as a result, we see the establishment of aesthetic distances as the most creative and liberating activity within all life's occasions. To be the artist of one's life involves the possibility of living within styles rather than within obsessions—that is, the possibility of repeating ourselves in an entertaining variety of performances rather than in the stultifying monotony of fantasies which break through each play of the self to be revealed as the boring "truth" of the self. A profound commitment to disguise (to what might even be labeled duplicity in an ethos of sincerity) is therefore perhaps essential for an exuberantly expansive self. *A la recherche du temps perdu* is certainly a novel about art, but it is not—as *Madame Bovary* is—a novel about the impossible distance between art and life; it is rather an inventory of techniques which make for a highly artful life.

 James M. Cox

AUTOBIOGRAPHY AND AMERICA

I

Autobiography and confessional writing are now receiving much more critical attention than they used to, and not merely because criticism has exhausted the other genres and is moving in on a relatively virgin field. For something has happened to the whole idea of literature in the last ten years. To remember that novelists such as Truman Capote and Norman Mailer have in *In Cold Blood* and *The Armies of the Night* challenged the distinction between nonfiction and fiction; to be reminded that biography and autobiography are more marketable products than fiction; to realize that *The Autobiography of Malcolm X* is somehow one of the great imaginative works of the last decade; to recall that Michel Butor told an MLA audience in Denver that there is no real difference between fiction and nonfiction, between a novel and an autobiography; and to know that a conference of an English Institute session was devoted to confessional literature—to reflect upon all this is to begin to acknowledge that much more has happened than a mere opportunistic exploitation of a neglected field.

Much of this change is, I think, a result of, and a response to, the revolutionary political attitudes and feelings which have fully emerged in the last five years. For when politics and history become dominant realities for the imagination, then the traditional prose forms of the essay and the autobiography both gain and attract power, and the more overtly "literary" forms of prose fiction—the novel and the short story—are likely to be threatened and impoverished. As such a process takes place—as politics and history tend to claim dominion over the imagination—then the literary imagination tends to respond by denying the generic distinctions which are both powerful and convenient categories in periods of stability and peace. Of course the problem is much more complicated, but these remarks may provide some sense of a present which can be related to my sense of the past importance of autobiography in America.

For autobiography has been important in this country. As I shall suggest, the very idea of autobiography has grown out of the political necessities and discoveries of the American and French revolutions. It is no mere accident that an astonishingly large proportion of the slender shelf of so-called American classics is occupied by autobiographies. Certainly *Walden* and *The Education of Henry Adams* would rank in almost anybody's list of the ten major American prose works, novels included. I would also include Franklin's *Autobiography*, though there would doubtless be dissenters as well as adherents to such a choice. Even so, I have chosen Franklin, Thoreau, and Adams primarily because they are central and not peripheral writers, are indeed classic American writers in the sense that their acts of imagination in the form of autobiography are unforgettable imaginative experiences. Whitman offers a problem which I shall face when I reach him.

II

So much for preliminaries. There remains the question of just what autobiography is—and despite the present tendency to blur generic distinctions, I want to try to keep them, and not simply as a convenience but as a necessary means of clarifying the whole subject. Strictly speaking, of course, autobiography is not a genre at all in the sense that poetry, fiction, and drama are. It is a term designating a subclass of that hopelessly confusing variety of writing we place under the heading of nonfictional prose. Yet of all the subclassifications in that inchoate group, autobiography and biography are probably the clearest in our minds. We at least think we know what we mean when we speak of autobiography and biography and we are equally sure that others mean the same thing when they speak of them. Thus, in answer to the question "What is autobiography?" I want to hold to the definition I believe we all know: a narrative of a person's life written by himself. Autobiography is in this sense the story of a life, but here there is a problem, for it is not the story but the history of a life, for it is history and not fiction—which raises the further issue of distinguishing between history and fiction. Without rushing to or yearning for conclusive definitions of the two, we can at least see that both history and fiction are at base narratives, the distinction being that one narrative is based on fact, the other on invention. The one tells a story of what did happen, the other of what did not; the one can be corroborated by public and private record, the other has to protect itself against the possibility of being taken literally. All this is of course commonplace, but it is often forgotten by critics of autobiography who begin to exercise the poetics of fiction in the analysis of autobiography.

There is another striking difference between the nature of historical and fictive narrative. In historical narrative the beginning and the ending are by necessity arbitrary and unreal (perhaps untrue would be the better term), for history has no beginning and no end. Thus the historian has to set up a principle of organization which will justify a beginning and an ending, concealing his intrusion into the irreversible historical stream. He therefore writes of the history of nations, of wars, of movements, of ideas, of governments, of decades, of explorations, always segmenting the continuous narrative line of history. His exit and entrance are the two sure fictive aspects of his form, and though he may achieve freedom of interpretation along the way, he is bound to the fact and the sequence of past events. The writer of fiction, on the other hand, has to begin and he has to end, for fiction is all invention, and its sure truths are that it does begin and does end. That is the inescapable necessity for the novelist and his whole effort is to realize that truth—to make the beginning and the ending as fatal and as final as they truly are.

Now autobiographical narrative falls between history and fictive narrative in this respect. If it is clearly historical in nature, it at least does have a beginning: the birth of its subject. True, the autobiographer, unless he has a prodigious memory, cannot remember his birth without becoming Shandean, but at least he can chronicle it from hearsay or he can begin with his first memory. In any event he has a point of beginning which is logical and incontrovertible, though of course he can deviate from such a point, beginning with a history of his parents, as if he were a biographer, or at an arbitrary point in his life almost as if he were a novelist. He cannot, however, write about his death. Thus that great event which is the goal of the biographer is forever inaccessible to the autobiographer, though he may establish a kind of pattern of his life which will enable him to treat it as if it were ended. There is another point which relates autobiography to fiction: autobiography is the life of a person, and both it and biography have subject matter which likens them to fiction, which is dependent on characters, that is, representations of persons.

These reflections, though they by no means define autobiography, do put us in a position to see rudimentary issues of autobiographical form. But there is also a historical problem about autobiography which is directly related to the subject of American autobiography. We are prone to think that autobiography preceded America, for if we know anything we know that there were great autobiographers before the American nation existed. St. Augustine, Cellini, Montaigne, and Casanova come quickly to mind. But it is a fact worth recording that autobiography as a term did not exist at the time of the American Revolution. It was first used, according to the OED, by Robert Southey in a review of Portuguese literature in 1809. Before the emergence of the term, there were two categories of people's lives written by themselves: the confession and the memoir. The confession was an account of a man's private life, centering on his emotions, feelings, secrets, frustrations—essentially his private world. The memoir was more on the order of chronicle, relating the individual's role upon the stage of history. The confession bared the inner thoughts; the memoir recounted the career. It is impossible to say just why autobiography should have emerged as a term to include both confession and memoir, but it may be helpful to note its appearance just after the age of revolution when the modern self was being liberated as well as defined. For the American and French revolutions, whatever else they did, were the convulsive acts which released the individual as a potent political entity and gave us what we are pleased to call modern man. And each nation produced in this revolutionary period a classic account of the self: Rousseau's *Confessions* and Franklin's *Memoir* (for Franklin had only the old term with which to name his book).

In this connection, it is worth noting that the corresponding classic in English literature of the period is a biography, Boswell's *Life of Johnson*. Thus, while America and France were readying for revolution, Franklin and Rousseau at almost the same moment in history were embarking on decisive accounts of themselves, while in England (which was desperately staving off revolution) Boswell was devoting himself to a biography of Johnson. Moreover, his relationship to his subject was constructed in terms of hierarchy. Yet if Boswell submitted to Johnson, Johnson in turn submitted himself to biography, and the completed work resulted in fulfillment for both men, since Boswell's remarkable revelation and recording of Johnson's talk raised Johnson's stature in English literature from a position of nobility to one of monarchy.

III

But Franklin and Rousseau were very great revolutionaries, and while Johnson was writing his pamphlet against the American Revolution (an act which Boswell regretted), they were engaged in liberating themselves in accounts of their own lives. These accounts were no mere records of their pasts, but genuine acts of life, not mere ways of saying but essential acts of being. Thus, Rousseau, after showing talent in a host of ways—as musician, social philosopher, pamphleteer, and novelist—at last liberated the self which stood behind yet could not be released by all the forms of expression he had tried. "I felt before I thought," he announced near the beginning of his *Confessions*, and his entire book was devoted to the generative life of feeling. The self which emerges in his pages is, with all its contradictions, something new and powerful in literature.

Instead of recording shame and later conversion in the manner of St. Augustine, Rousseau gives a nearly shameless revelation of himself, prefaced by a dare to all men to say whether they are better than he. Such a dare would be mere rhetoric if Rousseau in the course of his confessions did not exceed the wildest expectations of what an inner self might be. Thus, if his perversity and his revelations about his thwarted, devious, deviant, and frantic sexuality evoke surprise, his defenses of himself evoke outrage, and his pleas for justice by posterity are likely to provoke judgment and suppression on the part of those who wish for order. Small wonder that Johnson deplored Rousseau, for the self which Rousseau releases is the very self which Johnson's whole life was bent upon checking. Indeed Rousseau's release of such a self was the promise of the revolution which Johnson could feel in his very bones and which his whole style was both continuously and precariously subduing.

How different is Franklin's life. Johnson himself would have been hard put to disapprove it. Whereas Rousseau had released his inner life in the form of confession, Franklin chronicled his public life. Yet just as Rousseau had transformed the confession, Franklin transformed the memoir. Although Franklin chronicles his rise from obscurity to prominence, he does not suppress his emotional life so much as he shows the process of converting, using, and incorporating his desires, inner conflicts, doubts, and frustrations into a model life which in its turn can also be used by posterity. Thus, having organized a philosophical society, a university, a hospital, a lending library, an efficient postal system, and having invented the stove, the smokeless streetlamp, bifocals, electrical conduction, the harmonica, and a host of other items too numerous to mention, Franklin at the age of sixty-five embarked upon what one wants to call his greatest invention—the invention of himself, not as fiction, but as a fact both of and in history.

What is truly interesting is that Franklin's act of conceiving, discovering, or inventing himself almost exactly coincides with the birth of America. For Franklin began his biography in 1771 in England, just as he was becoming fully involved in the emerging separation from England, came back to work on it in France in 1784, worked on it again in 1788, and was once more involved with it months before his death in 1791. When he died, he had brought the record of his life forward to 1757—to that point when he was at the threshold of the professional diplomatic life, the life of his country, which would both occupy and preoccupy him for the rest of his days.

But Franklin is a true writer, and, like Rousseau, is as interested in the act of writing as in what he writes about. Thus he states at the outset that he is writing because he has a moment's time free from his diplomatic duties. He is therefore writing not simply out of leisure but as leisure, and that celebrated simple style of his with its even tenor equals the motive and act of leisure with which he begins. More than that, he sees his act of writing as the next best thing to living his life over again and he thus sees his memoir not as a record but as a second edition in which the sins of his life (which would have enormous emotional weight in the confessional form) become the mere errata of the first edition which he can point to and playfully wish to remove.

Even more important, he dates the time of his writing so that the dates of composition I referred to are not biographical information but textual reality. Thus the "life," which is to say Franklin's account of his early years, is placed between the years 1771 and 1788, the years of the American Revolution, confederation, and the Constitution. What literally happens in the form of Franklin's work is that the history of the revolution, in which Franklin played such a conspicuous part, is displaced by the narrative of Franklin's early life, so that Franklin's personal history *stands in place of the revolution.* Now the personal history which Franklin puts in place of revolutionary history recounts Franklin's rise from political anonymity and impotence to the position of agent for his colony, representing the people of Pennsylvania against the proprietors who reside in England. Thus, his life begins in Boston where freedom of the press is threatened by the crown and where freedom of impulse is threatened by his older brother; it ends in London where he is defending the colony from the attempted encroachments of the proprietors. But this represented history was not the actual revolution. There still remained the form which would realize the revolution and thus stand for it. That form was the autobiography—the life of a self-made, self-governing man written by the man himself. Though Franklin had only the term "memoir," it is not difficult to see why, in the light of what both he and Rousseau were doing to memoir and confession, a new term would be possible as well as necessary.

We can now turn to the structure of Franklin's autobiography to see how Franklin's history reveals the man. For Rousseau, life is total crisis; his life is defined in terms of one intense feeling after another. For Franklin, there is no crisis. For Rousseau, all life is a turning point, and he thus finds himself time after time insisting that such and such an event fixed his fate. For Franklin, there is no turning point; all events are essentially equal and that equality is not the mere inertness of a chronicle but a way of being which both reveals and reflects Franklin the man. Everything being essentially equal, Franklin is never trapped in or attached to events but free to see them with detachment and curiosity. Thus, because Franklin sees street drainage and street lighting as being equal to lawmaking and political theory, he is free from self-absorption as he walks home from assembly sessions to think about the possibility of inventions. His detached vision objectifies ideas, equalizes all concerns, and frees him to experiment with and concentrate upon a whole variety of probabilities.

Similarly, he is free in his form, for he makes use of the very limitations of the memoir. Thus he converts the limitation of being unable to catch up with his life and write of his death into the freedom of stopping his account whenever he wants to. After all, whenever he wants to or has to stop, for whatever reason whether business or death, will be the end. That of course is Franklin's freedom of form, and we do not find ourselves dissatisfied or wishing for more when Franklin does stop. He could have stopped with the first section of the book written in 1771 (he actually did stop and continued at the request of two Philadelphia friends, publishing their letters as a kind of advertisement of himself and his life) because he is not seeing his life in terms of turning point or finale, but as usable history: usable for others as a record of converting private desires into public life and private passions into rigorous self-government; usable for himself as leisure and amusement during a time of preoccupation with revolutionary duties. For the life he was able to recount in those few leisure moments was precisely that life which brought him to the fate of a career yet remained the old free experience in which he retained the possibility of doing everything or anything. Writing that life during the period when his career was fixed was not to recapture or relive the old free life (Franklin, unlike Rousseau, does not recall or remember or yearn for his past) but to assert that life as fact and put it in place of revolutionary history.

All this may seem like far-fetched speculation to those who wish to think that Franklin was just writing away on his life without any notion of writing a revolutionary book. Surely these speculations would at best amuse Franklin, but it is well in dealing with Franklin's consciousness to try to be as shrewdly calculating as he himself was. For Franklin knew he was going to be a revolutionary not only before the revolution but before he began his autobiography. Two weeks before he embarked upon the autobiography he wrote to James Otis, Thomas Cushing, and Samuel Adams one of the most visionary letters of the eighteenth century. Acquainting them with the repressive attitude of Parliament and the crown, he forecast the steps of the revolution which was to come:

I think one may clearly see, in the system of customs to be exacted in America by act of Parliament, the seeds sown of a total disunion of the two countries, though as yet that event may be at a considerable distance. The course and natural progress seems to be, first, the appointment of needy men as officers, for others do not care to leave England; then, their necessities make them rapacious, their office makes them proud and insolent, their insolence and rapacity make them odious, and, being conscious that they are hated, they become malicious; their malice urges them to a continual abuse of the in-

habitants in their letters to administration, representing them as
disaffected and rebellious, and (to encourage the use of severity) as weak, divided, timid, and cowardly. Government
believes all; thinks it necessary to support countenance to its
officers; their quarrelling with the people is deemed a mark
and consequence of their fidelity; they are therefore more
highly rewarded, and this makes their conduct still more insolent and provoking.

The resentment of the people will, at times and on particular incidents, burst into outrages and violence upon such officers, and this naturally draws down severity and acts of
further oppression from hence. The more the people are dissatisfied the more rigour will be thought necessary; severe punish-
ments will be inflicted to terrify; rights and privileges will be
abolished; greater force will then be required to secure execution and submission; the expense will become enormous; it will
then be thought proper, by fresh exactions, to make the people
defray it; thence the British nation and government will become odious, and subjection to it will be deemed no longer
tolerable; war ensues, and the bloody war will end in absolute
slavery to America or ruin to Britain by the loss of her colo-
nies; the latter most probable, from America's growing
strength and magnitude.

So Franklin not only saw the coming revolution, he calculated
the probable outcome. It may make him an unglamorous revolutionary to have had such vision, since one doesn't seem much
like a revolutionary if one has seen so much and calculated so
shrewdly. It is also worth remembering that Franklin was sixty-five when he determined upon revolution, an old age to
begin such an enterprise, but the fact may serve as a model of
possibility, a reminder that one doesn't have to be young, or
desperate, or hopeless to engage in a great revolution.

So of course Franklin's act of art in the *Autobiography* does not seem revolutionary; it seems even and easy and simple. But it is there in the path, and the best one can do to those Professors of English who condescend to it is to say simply and innocently that it is the first American book we have. For before Franklin there was no American literature; there was only English Colonial literature. With Franklin came consciousness, total consciousness in the form of autobiography—a history of a self-made life written by the man who made it. It is not a fiction but a cultural fact of life and we have to make the best of it.

IV

To make the best of it is to see the great American autobiography which followed not only in relation to Franklin's initial act but in relation to the history of the country. Here it is worth noting that Thoreau's *Walden*, by all admission the next great American autobiography, appears in 1854, at just the moment the nation was moving toward civil war, reminding us that autobiography becomes more possible when history and politics seem to possess the very drama we seek for in stage and fictive experience in periods of equanimity and peace. In any event, *Walden* did appear in 1854, and it was much concerned with the issues of slavery and abolition which were splitting the nation apart. But it was also autobiography, and Thoreau, like Franklin and Rousseau before him, was both revolutionary and writer. Thus, writing for him was as it was for them, not simply the record of experience but an act of life, a making of experience. Moreover, Thoreau, for all his differences from Franklin, does not turn inward upon himself or his feelings but looks out upon a world of natural fact. He too proposes a model life, and though it is not presented as a model to follow but one to equal, it is a life which Thoreau, like Franklin before him, has made for himself.

Yet this model life is much more than a making or recording of experience. It was for Thoreau a finishing of experience, and Thoreau's experiment in form is most dramatically evident in his determination to reach a conclusion, thereby completing his life—just what Franklin and Rousseau, by virtue of their choice of form, cannot do. There is a cost, of course, for Thoreau in order to complete his life has to take a part of it— the two years he spent at Walden Pond ten years earlier— and make that part stand for the whole. He went much further. He compressed the two years into one, letting the cycle of the seasons stand for the completed circle of the self. In order to make his style realize such a conception of the self, Thoreau sought a language at once metaphoric and concise. Yet for all the wit and concision of his language, there is always the fact of Walden Pond, a fact which lies outside himself and outside language as both a seal and a promise of his own reality. Much as Thoreau may play upon the analogies of the pond to his own life, its existence as a natural fact is as important for him as it is for us. That is why we cannot imagine Walden being a fiction, even though when we visit it today we inevitably realize that we did not really have to go there.

What Thoreau aimed to do was to translate the particular fact of Walden into the possibilities of being himself. Working steadily along analogical lines with that startling clarity of his, he saw himself as much a metaphor of Walden as it was of him. Because it was a pond, because it was self-contained, because it had the purity and clarity to reflect his image against the heavens, it became the reservoir of possibilities he could realize only in relation to it. The cycle of the seasons brooding over it was the natural time in which he determined to cast his life. And the hut he began to construct along its shores in the spring, occupied on July 4, and closed in with the coming of the ice upon Walden, gains significance always in relation to the pond which Thoreau, true surveyor that he was, maps and scrutinizes even as it reflects the self.

The self which emerges from the analogy is a far cry from the selves Franklin and Rousseau had discovered. Franklin, in concentrating on the externality of his past, had shown largely by implication in his style and structure the conversion of his inner self into a social and political self. Thus his "success" is an exemplary narrative implicitly depicting the sublimation of private energies into social action. Rousseau's experiential narration is almost the inverse of Franklin's. He discloses his progressive alienation from society—the long process by which he withdrew by stages from society to his island in a lake. His island is a perfect equivalent of the embattled, moated, insular present consciousness which at once generates and releases the past which has grown inside him.

For all their difference in self-conception, however, both Rousseau and Franklin realize themselves narratively and chronologically. In *Walden*, both narration and chronology tend to disappear, for just as a single year is being made to stand for a whole life, essence is always taking precedence over existence. Thoreau is neither taking over nor withdrawing from society. He stands between it and the pond in a constant attitude of seeing in Walden—Earth's Eye—an image of himself austerely and severely against society. That severity becomes Thoreau's fierce irony and makes the reading of *Walden* a humiliating as well as an exhilarating experience. The exhilaration comes from the kind of joy and independence Thoreau achieves in his insular solitude beside the pond. The humiliation comes from his almost savage criticism and exposure of the condition of man in his own time, and by ruthless implication, in all time to come. For Thoreau challenges his reader like a persecuting conscience. He says at the beginning that he writes not for the strong and self-reliant souls, if such there be, but for those who find themselves somehow unhappy with their lot. He shows in the course of his revolutionary life the possibilities which lie near at hand—as near and as familiar as Walden—but he also exposes the shabby lot society has made of life, revealing in a way that no other book has revealed not only that we can do what we want but that, alas! we have already done what we wanted—that as Americans we are always free to be free but that also as Americans we always choose to be slaves. That is why he brilliantly begins with the chapter on economy, showing the minimal requirements not simply for survival but for fulfillment. For Thoreau, writing almost on the eve of the Civil War, sees freedom not as Franklin's self-making but as self-possession. And he sees the self not as a means but as an end. Thus, unlike Franklin and Rousseau, he does indeed have a conclusion in which the self is completed in an ecstasy of possibility, a radiance and radiation of analogy and metaphor.

Yet Thoreau does not reach a conclusion so much as he is all conclusion, and his language is not a means to relate his history so much as it is itself his very essence—the literal translation of his being into symbol. That is why his whole direction is not to naturalize himself but to spiritualize nature, to overcome and subdue it, thereby becoming an ideal which will both afflict and elevate his reader. His language, his whole act of writing, is bent always toward a finish, a refinement, and a purity (in the full and not the genteel meaning of those words). In order to achieve a representative life, one which will stand for a complete life, Thoreau accentuates his individ-

uality. The tension in his consciousness and his style is thus always between universality and eccentricity, for in order to
dramatize the universality of the individual, Thoreau empha-
sizes the uniqueness of the self. His equivalent act in language
is to take such a personal hold of it that its abstractions are
bent to his will and wit. Insofar as he determines to represent
man he means to render a concrete life different from the lives
of others. The very burden of being an individual is to discover one's own way, which of necessity must take the individual to a land as distant, as austere, and as self-contained as
the Walden Pond he keeps discovering. These are the terms as
well as the burden of Thoreau's self-possession.

All this is of course self-evident, and I would not think of
claiming freshness of insight into *Walden*. To approach such
insight I need the presence of Whitman. I know that his presence in my list of autobiographers must seem anomalous. It is
anomalous, for Whitman is a poet if he is anything, and to
begin to play fast and loose with categories is to begin to play
the devil. If autobiography is narrative and history, then it is
not poem and prophecy. So my chief aim is not to claim
Whitman as autobiographer, but to use him to gain a perspective on Thoreau. Yet I cannot forbear a few defenses of having
included him. After all, he did write a poem entitled "Song of
Myself," which, considered in relation to Wordsworth's *Prel-
ude* and Coleridge's *Biographia Literaria*, reminds us how per-
vasive the autobiographical form in literature became after the
American and French revolutions. Moreover, Henry James,
Jr., in reviewing Whitman's poetry, said that whatever Whitman's medium was, it wasn't poetry, though he went on to observe that it wasn't prose either. As far as James could make
out in that early review (he happily lived to revise his opinion), Whitman's poetry was an incredibly vulgar offense

against the muse herself, a blatant exhibition of self which no one concerned with the craft and glory of art could condone. Art for James was a subduing of the self through form and language. James's criticism is still remarkably apt for anyone who hasn't genteelized Whitman with respectability, for Whitman is and should be hard to take. Instead of the fine economy we find in Thoreau's language, the wit, the intelligence, the precision, the exactness, there is a great deal of wind, flatness, and abstraction. There is much, much more, to be sure, but one of the feelings that Whitman's poetry inspires and clearly means to inspire is that we the readers could do as well—that, indeed, if this is poetry, then what isn't?

Thoreau had sought to create a sharply individualized consciousness which would stand for the possibilities of self-possession and had announced at the outset that though the first-person pronoun was dropped in many a personal narrative he would retain it. Whitman went another way. Seizing upon the crucial fact that in the pronominal system of the English language there is no distinction in form between the second-person singular and plural, he was able to address his reader as *you* and be at once personal and general. He added to that radical formal discovery an audacious democratic program of asserting an identification between the "I" of the poet and the "you"—both singular and plural—of all whom his poetry would prophesy. Whereas Thoreau's direction had been to translate his flesh into spirit and himself into concrete metaphor, Whitman's inspiration was to speak the word of himself, thereby creating the reader as poet. The reader would be the concrete emotional self, the embodiment of the word. Thus Thoreau's austerity and solitude; thus Whitman's constant emphasis upon love and union.

Considered in relation to their time, Whitman is the poet of

union, Thoreau the voice of secession, the most powerful voice
of secession in our literature. I do not mean that Thoreau was
a Southerner at heart. He wasn't. He was a Yankee, but Yan-
kees had been old revolutionaries, and revolution had meant
separation from authority. It took the genius of Lincoln to
transform the old revolutionary impulse toward separation,
which was as deep a part of American identity as the wish for
union, into a national will for union, and it took a bloody civil
war to establish the Union as an irrevocable reality. It is
hardly surprising in this connection that Thoreau should have
died quietly while the war raged in the South and that Whitman, who was totally prepared for the Civil War, could go to
the battlefields and hospitals as a male nurse, could kiss the soldiers of the South as well as those of the North, could—best
of all—write letters home for the wounded and dying, could
fully see Lincoln from the moment he took the stage (even
Emerson could hardly see him), and could write "When Lilacs
Last in the Dooryard Bloom'd" almost the moment Lincoln
was assassinated. If Milton had moved from elegy through losing civil war toward epic, Whitman moved from epic through
victorious civil war toward elegy, translating the dead bodies
of all his brave soldiers into the leaves of grass whose roots (as
he had epically promised in 1855) came out of the faint red
roofs of the mouths of the dead. The leaves of grass were nothing less than the living tongues of the dead. For if love was the
impulse which would create the future reader, death had to be
the event which Whitman had to translate. How else could
there be immortality of the flesh? For it is not immortality of
the spirit which interests Whitman—any Baptist preacher
could indulge that argument—but immortality of the flesh.
Thus, that magnificent line near the end of "Song of Myself":

> I effuse my flesh in eddies and drift it in lacy jags.

And thus the pun on leaves of grass as leaves of the book.

To face that pun fully is to remember Walden once more. For in Thoreau's chapter on Spring, just before his conclusion, he describes the breaking up of the ice on Walden and the thawing of the frozen earth. Standing before the railroad bankside which man has cut in nature, Thoreau sees the spring rivulets tenderly eroding the fresh earth and forming miniature alluvial fans whose shape takes the forms of primordial leaves. Playing upon the analogy, Thoreau sees earth's whole excretory process as a purification into, and a promise of, the leaves to come. Almost like a savage, he tries to make a language from the very word "leaf," expanding it into "lobe," gutterally evolving it further into "globe," and at last wishing that Earth's primal form will be translated into the leaves of his book so that he can turn over a new leaf at last. Just as the excretion of the world's body becomes the delicate leaf above the earth, Thoreau wants his words and pages to be the purification of his flesh into pure spirit, a resurrection of the body. Whitman on the other hand, seeks to say and be the word which will descend into the body, and his urge as well as his vision is literally to embrace the world and become it, to embrace reader and readers and become them, to be the tongue which invades every part of the body and gives every part an equal voice—a radical democratization of both body and body politic and an immortal union of himself with the world of readers he is creating, so that "Song of Myself" will, when we begin to grasp it, be true to its title—the song of ourselves, the instantaneous miracle which makes us poets, putting us at the threshold of a living faith that, lo and behold, we are the living poem which Whitman's new biblical verse has created.

V

It is a long way from Thoreau and Whitman to Henry Adams, largely because Adams himself sought to make the space in time as wide as possible. Yet differently as he saw and created his life from theirs, like them he eschews the confessional element in autobiography. He does not remember, explain, or defend his past in the manner of Mill and Newman any more than he wishes to confess and reveal it in the manner of Rousseau, but, like Franklin and Thoreau, he makes use of it and makes it useful. His too is a model life, but not a paradigm like Franklin's or a challenge like Thoreau's, for his whole notion of a model life is that of a manikin—a figure in which clothing, outline, and pattern are everything, the life nothing but plaster and sawdust, an elusive and ironic joke at the center of education, which is at once history, the thought into which life has died, and art, the narrative upon which life is spent. Being a historian, Adams saw life as history; being an autobiographer, he knew he had to make life art. Being these and being an Adams, too, he dared to identify his history with that of his country. Comprehending these strands of being in a single narrative, he left an autobiography which drew life from the autobiography that had gone before him and abundantly gave meaning back to it, as I shall try to demonstrate.

There are two striking facts of form in Adams's *Education*. First, it is written in the third person and therefore guarantees the possibility of completeness. Second, it has a gap in the center, a vacuum of twenty years about which Adams hardly speaks. We know—and such a fact of form forces us to wonder if we don't know—what happened during those twenty years. He taught at Harvard (he touches upon this fact) and was therefore not a student of life. He wrote history (he alludes to this at points along his way) and was thus a historian instead of being a part of history. And he married, only to experience the tragedy of his wife's suicide (he alludes only once to that harrowing event, telling of watching in Rock Creek Cemetery the people who came to see Saint-Gaudens's great sculpture of grief which monumentalized his wife's grave). These three acts are the silence in the midst of life, and the autobiography which surrounds them is the act of mind converting them into their opposite. The teacher is converted into the student Henry Adams; the historian is converted into the victim and expression of history. And the grief-stricken husband is converted into the pleasure seeker of the mind whose whole act of play is to convert his past into a third person in an act of joyful suicide.

To see these paradoxes is to begin to grasp the consequences of Adams's third-person narration, consequences which Adams embraces with almost dismaying enthusiasm. Thoreau had retained the "I" but in order to achieve a completed self was forced into the synecdochic strategy of making a part stand for the whole. Adams, however, by converting himself into the third person was able to treat himself not as character— for characters are in fiction and drama, not in autobiography —but as history. The consequences of such a strategy are enormous. For if the self is truly history, then it is somehow past, and Adams would become merely the biographer of himself. Yet Adams is not a biographer but an autobiographer, and of all things the *Education* is not, one is surely biography. It is rather a division of the self into two parts, two poles—a past and a present—in which the present self generates the past self as history. The new Henry Adams, the present generative consciousness, which in conventional historical terms grew out of the past, is by virtue of Adams's inversion actually releasing and attracting the old Henry Adams (he would be the young Adams in conventional terms) toward his source. Adams fully realizes these inversions by means of a style which can best be described as a series of paradoxes riding upon a narrative current.

The new Adams, the present Adams, who is as much the source as the end of the past, constantly exposes the descent of the old Adams, who, born too late into history from a line of Presidents and fated for success and power, steadily failed. The old Adams, always unprepared for contingency, is drawn forward—not recorded or chronicled—through the resistance of history toward the moment of the present which is the hidden "I" that he can never reach. That is the fate of Adams's form which casts the self as history. The old Adams's approach to the present is as a victim of forces beyond his control, a child amid theory, politics, technology, and, above all, accelerating history. Everything he is made to learn merely unprepares him for the past through which he is drawn. He is the great-grandson and the grandson of Presidents only to feel himself cast aside from the sources of power; he goes to Harvard only to discover himself a fool in Europe; he faces the Civil War as a loyal Union man only to discover that the real treason was the betrayal of his father by Charles Sumner, the most trusted family friend; he goes to England as secretary for his father the ambassador in an effort to secure the balance of power they think England holds only to discover that the Civil War has already shifted the power to America and that England by remaining neutral has actually fallen behind history; he learns evolution only to return to America and find Grant in the White House; he attempts to expose the economic scandals of the Grant era only to find himself in touch with the energy of capital—which defies all his calculations;

he teaches medieval history at Harvard only to discover his total ignorance of all history; he writes the history of the early years of the Republic only to recognize that the ideas of humanistic history are completely negated by the laws of physical energy. And so at last he attempts to learn the laws of science in an effort to plot force and energy in time, thereby making the art of history a science possessing predictive force, only to realize that acceleration is the law of history. Having made his predictions and seen the law of acceleration, he steps aside.

This series of belated recognitions constitutes the history and the failure of the old Adams, but it is failure generated by the polarity of the new Henry Adams in relation to the old. Indeed, the new Adams is literally *educating* the old Adams, giving the title an active and present sense which is often overlooked. Moreover, he is educating him all the time, at every instant of the narrative. For the education is nothing less than the act and vision whereby the new Adams ironically objectifies the old as a victim of history. If the old Adams is being educated by the new, the discovery is not simply one of gloomy personal failure but of the failure of all the history he has lived through—the dissolution of an old order of causation into a new energy. Thus the nineteenth century dissolves into the twentieth, exposing in the process the fact that the men of power—thinkers, politicians, and diplomats—were not simply wrong but did not even know what they were doing, were indeed victims of the power and drift of history. Their ignorance was but one more mass of energy for the historian to measure in terms of its force.

As the old Henry Adams is attracted toward the new, his life is taken not as a loss or grief but as a conversion, and not the conversion of confessional form—the conversion of man into God as in Augustine, or into feeling as in Rousseau—but a conversion into historical force, so that autobiographical narrative does not displace history, as in Franklin, but becomes an ironic vision of history. The moment of conversion is, as everyone knows, Adam's vision of the dynamo in the gallery of machines at the Paris exposition of 1900, six hundred years after Dante's vision of Beatrice. The dynamo is the beautiful objectification of Adams's act of form, for it comes into being at precisely the moment when the old Henry Adams has been attracted to the present source of his energy. True to his form at this moment when he envisions the dynamo as the end of the old Adams, the new Adams is able to see an opposite force, not forward in time but backward in history; he sees the Virgin.

These then become the poles of past and future which the old and the new Adams generate as they meet at the beginning of the twentieth century; they are at the same time the poles of energy which constitute Adams's conversion, for they make possible his dynamic theory and act of history. Because it is at once theory (an analytic formulation about past and future) and act (a literal attraction of the old Adams to the source which has generated him) it can become a genuine vision, but a vision in Adamic not in Augustinian terms, for it is a conversion of the self not into divine but into historical lines of force. That is why Adams's vision of the future is not so much prophetic as it is speculative.

Happily for us, the poles of dynamo and Virgin are also beautifully conclusive as a vision of autobiography and America. For Adams's discovery of the dynamo takes us directly back to our point of departure. After all, Franklin not only invented American autobiography; he also discovered—fathered might be the better term—electricity, and those

Promethean acts bind him deeply to Adams's form and substance. More than that, there was an old family score for Adams to settle, and though Adams was terribly ironic about himself and his progenitors, he *was* an Adams through and through and had a way of dealing with the Jeffersons and Randolphs who had thwarted his great-grandfather. Franklin in Paris during the American Revolution had driven John Adams to distraction with his social ease, detachment, and wit. While John Adams toiled, Franklin seemed to play and yet reap all the praise. The whole miserable contrast so piqued Adams that he confided his exasperation to his journal. So in disclosing the dynamo as the essence of America and the future which would be American, Henry Adams was evening old scores even as he was being utterly true to his form. If Franklin had seen autobiography as self-generation, Adams would show the end of self-generation. Instead of seeing his life as the rise from obscurity to prominence, Adams saw it as the descent from prominence into obscurity and utter posthumous silence. Instead of treating life as a chronicle of success, Adams showed it as both the history of failure and the failure of history. Thus at the moment of his conversion, the old Adams feels like worshipping the dynamo, but the new Adams generates the opposite of the dynamo—the Virgin of a deeper, more primal past. For what autobiography as self-generation perforce left out was woman, the force which had moved the medieval world in Adams's illuminated vision of the past, and yet the force which had been rendered irrelevant by American autobiography and revolution. There were no women in Franklin's world of the self-invented self—only the wife as helpmeet in the most practical sense and as a practical object for excess sexual energy. There were no women at all in Thoreau's world. Although there was a feminine principle in Whitman, he hermaphroditically absorbed it as he absorbed Kanada and Missouri and Montana.

And so Adams delightfully chose the Virgin, not at all as a converted Catholic, possibly as atonement and love for the wife who had killed herself, certainly as a pleasure seeker in history where he could be a tourist to his heart's desire.

All this is much, but it is not all. Adams declared an end to education, autobiography, and history in 1905, the year John Hay concluded the treaty between Russia and Japan. That marked the end of Adams's old eighteenth-century provincial America, the America of Franklin's invention. That America had moved from peripheral and provincial entity to become *the* treaty-making power in the West, and thus a line of force to meet the inertia of Russia and China in the East. Thus, the city which had drawn his ancestors from Quincy and Boston and which Adams, having failed to occupy as President had occupied as historian, was now the center of power in the West—the point from which Adams could let the energy of his mind run its own lines of force into the past and future.

But there is still more. The year 1905 was the date of Einstein's equation and the beginning of all that it has meant. Though Adams may not have known the equation, after reading the *Education*, who can say that he could not have imagined it? Even to ask the question is to answer it, for the fact is that Adams's *Education* is the heroic act of the imagination unifying history and science in an act of mind and art. To read it is to recognize the genuine pathos of C. P. Snow's cry of alarm, some fifty years later, at the perilous division between the two cultures of science and the humanities. Whatever its content, the form of Snow's "scientific" vision is, like his forms of fiction, still in the age of Howells. Adams had not only seen and measured the division between the two cultures, but had imagined them as the poles of attractive force which, converting the inertia of life and history into energy of mind, would transform the self into a unifying consciousness—a third force in a new magnetic field. That is why his book is genuinely true to its title, remaining to this day an education for *any* twentieth-century reader. Of all American literature, it alone deserves to be required reading for all *students*, which is far from saying that it should be required reading for everyone or that it is the "best" American autobiography.

VI

This, however, is an essay not about education but about American autobiography, and Adams's achievement puts me in a position to conclude the subject, which does not mean to summarize my argument. A conclusion, it seems to me, ought to evoke an American writer after Adams who somehow extended the American autobiographical tradition along the lines of force I have tentatively sketched out.

For me, that writer is Gertrude Stein. She is the woman whom Adams had tried to imagine emerging from the American scene. She drops out of medical school and the world of philosophy and science to become a dictatorial force in the world of art. She realizes almost from the beginning that America is not the newest but the oldest country in the world, since, immediately following its own Civil War, it was the first country fully to enter the modern world of steam and electricity. She leaves America to occupy Paris, the city of art, there to become an aesthetic dictator of the new art which, emerging from the nineteenth-century dissolution of image and representation into impression, asserted clarity of line in an instantaneous perspective of abstraction. And she was, inevitably, an autobiographer. But where Adams had, by doubling himself, succeeded in retaining a narrative past at once generated by and attracted to a present consciousness, Gertrude Stein sought an absolute present in which not the life would be everything, the words nothing—as in Whitman—but the words everything and the life nothing. The abstraction of language would be the total present, and the achievement of the writer would lie in disconnecting language from referential reality, thereby making the words upon the page not true but real, not possessed of but possessing total reality in and of themselves. They would, in her words, be "being existing."

The only way that Gertrude Stein could even acknowledge narrative existence was to write through her companion Alice B. Toklas speaking about herself. Thus, like the other American autobiographers she could only reach herself by going outside. In reaching herself by being, not imagining, her intimate companion, she was not at all trying to gain an objective perspective on herself. Instead, she was uniting both autobiographical and biographical consciousness in a single creative act, thereby annihilating their priority and leaving only anecdotal perception upon the page as pure act and pure fact— not a new life in time, but a new existence in space. It has been said that she became her own Boswell, and in a sense she did, but it might be truer to say that, after writing *The Making of Americans*, she at last became one. Perhaps it was right that she should have settled in Paris, the city where Franklin had gone—in D. H. Lawrence's vision—to cut a hole in the Old World through which Europe would eventually bleed to death. Lawrence, at the end of his essay on Franklin written between the wars when Hitler was waiting in the wings of history, had cried out for Europe to let hell loose and get its own back from America. But when Hitler finally did let hell loose, it was certainly right that Gertrude Stein, who had been in Paris all those years, should have been waiting there to receive the victorious American soldiers when they liberated the city in 1945.

She—as American, as man-woman, as new Buddha—seems to me to be both the fact and the mystery at the end of American autobiography. Her life in time, which ended in 1946, a year after the atomic bomb, is a good place to end this glimpse of the subject. Her life in words, a total present, would be the living fact on which to base a genuine vision of American autobiography as American history. That is why she is my conclusion.

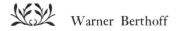 Warner Berthoff

WITNESS AND TESTAMENT:
TWO CONTEMPORARY CLASSICS

Matter of interest for literary historians: have any recent American books made a stronger impression on the consciousness of people who read literature than *The Autobiography of Malcolm X*, published posthumously in 1965, and *The Armies of the Night*, Norman Mailer's chronicle of the Pentagon march published in 1968?

Characteristically both books seem part and parcel of the civil turbulence of the past decade in American life. To speculate at this point in time about their ultimate place in literary history may seem the least bit precious. Yet to speak of them merely as books having a considerable civil and topical importance, or even as documents whose testimony has already imposed itself on our understanding of our time's singular history, is to do less than full justice to the literary achievement they embody. Calling them "classics" is not just pitchman's slang. I am simply persuaded that these two books do in fact have a central place in the continuing major history of Ameri-

can writing; that they are works of formed imaginative argument as powerfully developed and sustained as any we have
had during the past quarter century; works organized and
deepened by imaginative conceptions of the story to be told
which have in the end not only a tough interior truthfulness
but also, emerging as determining themes, a visionary force, a
transforming authority. And what precisely do we mean by
high literature if not work of this character?

Both books are aggressively personal in focus and, like much
current poetry, confessional in their tactics of statement. At
the same time they are books which quite obviously first won
a hearing, and are fixtures now in the paperback market, by
reason of their topicality. The two authors in their different
ways have been public men with a vengeance; and what they
write about in these books are matters as central to the public
life of our time as any we can think of—the black revolt, the
fight against the Vietnam War, and all that each signifies in
the moral and civil history of American society. Thus we are
likely to respond to them in rather special ways. We may in-
tensely *want* to find them forceful and impressive; we feel that
they could be weapons, each one, in a great cause. We may
read them therefore with a certain indulgence. We ask them
only to be just good enough, to give what encouragement
they can to struggles which we know will not be won merely
by writing and reading books.

A great many books have recently been claiming our attention in this way; and it is of special interest that literary men
(and women) have been drawn into writing them, as if to satisfy some new, or revived, test of occupational seriousness. So
we find an old-school man of letters like Robert Penn Warren
turning out a collection of interviews on segregation and race
consciousness; a book it is possible to think as nicely fitted to

Warren's raconteur's talent as any he has ever given us. From a younger novelist, Jeremy Larner, comes one of the livelier accounts of Eugene McCarthy's campaign in 1968; from Susan Sontag, an impressive report on the impact of a visit to North Vietnam. Those novels and poems, too, that show some special boldness of ambition are likely to have, or move toward, the form of public statement—like Saul Bellow's latest novel, *Mr. Sammler's Planet*, or Joyce Carol Oates's *Expensive People* ("a hatchet," says her narrator, "to slash through my own heavy flesh and through the flesh of any one else who happens to get in the way"), or Robert Kelly's "long poem about America in time," *The Common Shore*, of which the opening section is called with proper ominousness, "The State of Siege."

Black writers especially seem compelled to accommodate their effort as writers to public, civil ends. More or less inevitably their books are received as public documents first of all, and perhaps they come to be written out largely according to that expectation. (Black North American writers, that is, as against those from black Africa and the West Indies, who in the main seem freer to be read and to think of themselves as primarily novelists, dramatists, poets.) Thus it was with particular regard to black American writers and books that the critic Richard Gilman formulated, not long ago, an argument concerning the kind of writing I am discussing, and the response proper to it, that touches directly on my present concern. Mr. Gilman was addressing himself to Eldridge Cleaver's *Soul on Ice*, another best-seller for topical reasons, and the critical line he took was deliberately provocative. With such books, he said, the first thing we professional readers of literature have to do is suspend altogether our ordinary standards. In a word, these books are not for us. The conditions under which they are written are conditions of constraint and desperation literally unimaginable to non-blacks; and the special service they perform for their authors and for the community of black readers is such that our trained habits of judgment simply do not apply—*cannot* apply—and must be discarded, being not only inappropriate but in present circumstances socially and humanly destructive. *Soul on Ice* is not just another work of literature; it is nothing less than "an act of creation and definition of the self" on the part of a man totally estranged from us and our cultural privileges and assumptions. We have indeed, as Mr. Gilman nicely puts it, to "make room" for *Soul on Ice*, "but not on the shelves we have already built." [1]

Now this argument (from a critic whose general good sense I very much respect) can be criticized in various ways. Sociological and, in a fashion, philosophical ways, chiefly. If books like *Soul on Ice* derive from civil and psychological conditions so vastly different from those assumed by standard literary criticism, if they represent an act of mind so remote from ordinary literary performance, will anything such criticism chooses to say make a difference one way or another? Will it in fact keep these books from doing their special job? Or will their authors really be beaten into silence and their proper readers turned away by comments that by definition are so immensely irrelevant? Also, wouldn't this argument apply equally to other special classes of books? Mr. Gilman himself, in correspondence following his essay, sensibly acknowledged the force of objections that the same sort of thing may be said of women's literature, books by women about the special experience of women in our society, or of the literature of homo-

[1] Gilman's essay, and a further reply to some of his critics, are reprinted in his collection, *The Confusion of Realms* (New York, 1970).

sexuality or of criminality. (How much we would lose, for example, if Genet's writing was automatically exempted from critical interrogation.) Mr. Gilman might have been challenged even more centrally, I think, by reference to the literature of religious experience and religious indoctrination; the work, for instance, of an author like Thomas Merton, whose liberating influence Eldridge Cleaver very handsomely acknowledges in his book. Here in particular the writer's work is subordinated to doctrinal and sectarian purposes, and most frequently represents or symbolizes just such an act of self-creation and self-definition. But have we really no way of discriminating objectively between Thomas Merton and, say, Mary Baker Eddy, or in a nineteenth-century context between Mrs. Eddy's writing and Newman's or Kierkegaard's, with regard to the discursive authority each possesses and to both the mediate and ultimate consequences of an absorption in them? Most broadly, is it really impossible to enter imaginatively, rationally, the world of discourse of people whose outlook and life-experience are substantially different from our own, and whose stake in the making of books differs correspondingly? Isn't Mr. Gilman's argument at some point profoundly patronizing? Does it mean anything that the suspension of critical valuation it calls for would be especially suitable to children's writing or to the writing-for-therapy of the mentally sick?

The matter would be interesting to thrash out on these grounds; it could lead into wide-ranging sociological, perhaps political, debate. But the objection I particularly want to make is more strictly literary, though not for that reason less serious. Mr. Gilman's argument seems to me characteristic of a good deal of well-intentioned concern these days with the matter of "relevance," the relevance of traditional disciplines of thought to present social needs; a form of it crops up all around the mass of current writing and thinking about the teaching of English in schools and colleges. It involves, I suspect, a strangely limited understanding of what constitutes the species "literature" and of what is involved in the consideration of literary "form"—to leave aside its curious historical forgetfulness about the whole main set of the Romantic and post-Romantic ethos, that great rallying ground of the anticlassical, antihierarchical "confusion of realms" that Mr. Gilman has taken as his critical theme.

To quote him again, "we have all considered that the chief thing we should be working towards" in literary criticism is a certain state of "disinterestedness," of " 'higher' truth and independent valuation," and so forth; but who precisely is this "we"? in what cork-lined chamber of adjudication does this "we" hang out? Am I right in detecting here the presence, as a main term of argument, of an odd parochial confusion in understanding and applying the modernist dogma of the "autonomy" of literature; some queer residue of the classroom rigors of the famous "new criticism" and the legendary purity of its disregard for questions of intention, effect, social implication? Mr. Gilman's argument turns, I think, on a position I doubt he himself would tolerate for a moment—on a strict separation of "literature" and the considerations appropriate to it from *any* writing done in the service of extraliterary causes or having a direct social or personal end, or from any consideration of the part such purposes commonly play in major literary history.

On this, two general points might be made. One is that the more we look into the matter the more we see that all modern literary creation (in ways determined by the whole supporting culture) involves just such acts of self-creation and self-definition; a point it would be entertaining to develop with refer-

ence to some entirely respectable case like that of Milton, who
had a good deal to say about the personal factor in high literary achievement, the noble infirmity of wanting to make a
name for yourself, and so on. In American writing in particular, where Emerson, Whitman, Hart Crane remain archetypal
presences, this motivational confusion of realms, of craftsman-
ship and soulmaking, has been of the central stuff of working
tradition. In any event the question is not of totally disparate
categories of performance, out of reach of each other's standards of valuation, but of different histories, or circumstances,
or doctrines and conceptions, of "the self"; different working
postures and strategies, adopted according to each writer's picture of his own and his audience's situation; different expressive intentions embraced and different effects sought, each
having its own reasonable measure of virtue. The other general
point is that writing meant to serve directly some social cause
or personal end will do so more effectively by creating, so to
speak, a broad or an intense imaginative field of reference and
allusion—and will therefore also have its distinctive resources and precedents in past expressive tradition; for such
fields of reference and allusion are not created out of raw sensation or an unsupported will. If these are not literary resources and precedents, what are they?

The particular forms writing of this kind commonly uses are
familiar enough: the open letter, the preachment, the apology,
the parable or representative anecdote, the capitulatory brief,
the tirade, the narrative or polemical exposé, the public prayer,
the appeal to conscience, the call to arms. These are the literary forms in fact, forms mostly of direct address designed not
only to reach but in a sense to *create* a genuine audience, that
Soul on Ice is written in; the forms, too, that for obvious reasons have traditionally been most available in the social com-

munity Eldridge Cleaver's writing emerges from and largely assumes. (By this I mean not only the black community but the larger national community—the community *manqué*, not so much fragmented as fundamentally unformed—which since independence has been the immovable obstacle in the path of high American ambition, in literature and out of it.) The rhetoric or style Eldridge Cleaver works in corresponds. It is, quite simply, a version of that long-established plain style of first-person deposition and affirmation in which so much of modern revolutionary polemic and testimony on the non-Marxist side has been cast. (Rousseau, Tom Paine, Voltaire are among a sizable company of predecessors and models cited by the in fact quite noticeably bookish author of *Soul on Ice*, though a nearer source would be popular oratory and evangelical preaching.) And it seems to me that an exercise of specifically literary criticism—formal, stylistic—is altogether appropriate to books of this kind, though it may require kinds of discretion and informed good sense that are not guaranteed possessions among graduates of our organized critical schooling. It strikes me as very much worth knowing, and worth saying in the right way, whether a writer like Eldridge Cleaver uses the received modes he has chosen to write in well or badly—and by "well" I mean adroitly, cogently, mindopeningly. It is a *critical* finding which, if reached in a way that makes sense to us, may provide a useful pragmatic measure of the present strength and tactical readiness of the whole collective movement of mind, conscience, social will, which the book in question speaks for, and out of.

But to remind ourselves that these modes and forms do also properly belong to the history of literature is only to point up the disregard of them that has somehow got institutionalized among us. How prominent *is* Tom Paine in English or American literary studies? I am not sure that much room is ever made for him, in Mr. Gilman's figure, on the shelves we regularly work from or send our students to—or that we would quite know how to make the critical case for getting him up there. Yet Paine is one of the genuine masters of English prose in the plain or popular style, surely as much so as Burke is of its forensic opposite. (But that style, too, is neglected as an object of inquiry; we would hardly know how to begin to talk critically about it.) That being the case, we may have to agree, on practical grounds, that Mr. Gilman has a point; our common practice of literary criticism does not prepare us to deal very effectively with books like *The Rights of Man* or *Soul on Ice*.

In any event, since the matter applies a fortiori to Malcolm's autobiography, let us turn to that remarkable book.

No one can read very much of Malcolm's writing, more precisely listen to the voice transcribed in the autobiography (dictated to the journalist Alex Haley) or the printed versions of his public speeches, without forming the sense of an extraordinary human being: fiercely intelligent, shrewdly and humanely responsive to the life around him despite every reason in the world to have gone blind with suspicion and hate, a rarely gifted leader and inspirer of other men. The form of autobiographical narration adds something further; he comes through to us as the forceful agent of a life-history that was heroic in the event and has the shape of the heroic in the telling, a protagonist who (in Francis R. Hart's fine description) has himself created and now re-creates "human value and vitality in each new world or underworld he has entered." [2]

[2] "Notes for an Anatomy of Modern Autobiography," *New Literary History*, Vol. I, No. 3 (Spring, 1970).

The power of Malcolm's book is that it speaks directly out of the totality of that life-history *and* the ingratiating openness of his own mind and recollection to it. It seems to me a book that, *pace* Mr. Gilman, does not require any softening or suspension of critical judgment. In the first place it is written, or spoken, in a quick, pungent, concrete style, again the plain style of popular idiom, improved and made efficient by the same sort of natural sharpness and concentration of attention that gives life and color to the best of Mark Twain's recollective writing, or Franklin's, or Bunyan's. In the run of the narrative the liveliness of observation and recollection, the "histrionic exuberance" (Professor Hart again), are continuously persuasive—and incidentally confirm as elements of a true style Alex Haley's assurance that the book is indeed Malcolm's own and not a clever piece of mimicry or pastiche. The casually vivid rendering of other persons is worth remarking, a test some quite competent novelists would have trouble passing. People who were especially important to Malcolm—his strong-minded half-sister Ella; the motherly white woman who ran the detention home he was sent to at thirteen, who was always kind to him and would call his people "niggers" to his face without a flicker of uneasiness; Shorty from Boston, who set him up in business; West Indian Archie, who "called him out"; or the tough convict Bimbi in Charlestown prison, strange little man of unexpected thoughts and arguments, who broke through the wall of rage and hate Malcolm was closing around himself—all these figures are precisely defined, according to their place in the story. The grasp of the narrative extends in fact to whole sociologies of behavior. The Harlem chapters in general, with their explanation of hustling in all its major forms—numbers, drugs, prostitution, protection, petty in-ghetto thievery—offer one of the best accounts in our literature of the cultural underside of the American business system, and of the bitter psychology that binds its victims to it; Malcolm came to see very clearly how the habituations bred by ghetto poverty operate to destroy individual efforts to break out of it, and he could use that insight with force and point in his preaching. Most generally it is just this blending of his own life-story with the full collective history of his milieu and the laws of behavior controlling it that gives Malcolm's testimony its strength and large authority—and sets it apart, I think, from the many more or less skillfully designed essays in autobiography we have had recently from writers like Frank Conroy, Claude Brown, Norman Podhoretz, Willie Morris, Paul Cowan, David McReynolds, to mention only a few; sets it apart also from the great run of novels about contemporary city life.

But it is Malcolm himself, and his own active consciousness of the myth of his life's progress, that most fills and quickens the book, making it something more than simply a valuable document. His past life is vividly present to him as he speaks; he gives it the form, in recollection, of a dramatic adventure in which he himself is felt as the precipitating agent and moving force. It is not unreasonable that he should see himself as someone who has a special power to make things happen, to work changes on the world around him (and to change within himself); and thus finally as one whose rise to authority is in some sense in the natural order of things, the working out of some deep structure of fortune. That is my way of putting it; Malcolm himself, as a Muslim, of course uses other words.[3]

The force of this continuously active process of self-concep-

---

[3] So Borges: "A classic is that book which a nation (or group of nations, or time itself) has taken to read as if in its pages everything were predetermined, predestined, deep as the cosmos, and capable of endless interpretation" (*New York Review of Books*, August 13, 1970).

tion and self-projection is fundamental to the book's power of truth. It gives vitality and momentum to the early parts of the story, the picture of Malcolm's salad days as a Roxbury and Harlem sharpie, with conked hair and "knob-toed, orange-colored 'kick-up' shoes," the wildest Lindy-hopper and quickest hustler of all, delighting always in his impact on others—as in the interlude of his first trip back to Lansing, Michigan, to wow the yokels with his Harlem flashiness—finding satisfaction, too, in the names, the folk-identities, that attach to him at each new stage: "Homeboy," "Harlem Red" or "Detroit Red," "Satan" in the storming defiance of his first imprisonment. Most decisively, this force of self-conception is what brings alive the drama of his conversion, and his reemergence within the Nation of Islam as a leader and teacher of his people. For Malcolm's autobiography is consciously shaped as the story of an "education," and in so describing it I am not merely making the appropriate allusion to Henry Adams or the *Bildungsroman* tradition; "education" is Malcolm's own word for what is taking place.

Above all, the book is the story of a conversion and its consequences. We can identify in it various classic features of conversion narrative. A full detailing of the crimes and follies of his early life makes more astonishing the change of changes that follows ("The very enormity of my previous life's guilt prepared me to accept the truth"). In the central light of this new truth, particular events take on symbolic dimensions; they stand as the exemplary trials and challenges which the redeemed soul must pass through and by which it knows the meaning, feels the reality, of its experience. That meaning and reality, to repeat, are not merely personal. The outlines of grander historical patterns are invoked and give their backing to the story—the whole long history and tragedy of the black race in America; then, at the crisis, the radically clarifying mythology of the Black Muslim movement (a mythology which, to any one willing to consider it objectively, has the character of a full-blown poetic mythology; a source, once you place yourself inside it, of comprehensive and intrinsically rational explanations for the life-experience it refers to, that of the mass of black people in a historically racist society).

And always there is Malcolm's own fascination with what has happened to him, and what objectively it means. As if establishing a leitmotif, the climaxes of his story repeatedly focus on this extraordinary power to change and be changed that he has grown conscious of within himself and that presents itself to him as the distinctive rule of his life. Malcolm speaks with a just pride of his quickness to learn, to "pick up" how things are done in the world; of his readiness, even when it humiliates him, to accept schooling from those in possession of some special competence or wisdom; of a "personal chemistry" of open-mindedness and quick realism that requires him to find out the full vital truth of his own experience and that keeps it available to consciousness from that time forward. His curiosity about life is unquenchable ("You can hardly mention anything I'm not curious about"). He has a driving need to understand everything that happens to him or around him and to gain a measure of intelligent control over it; it is a passion with him to get his own purchase on reality.

It thus makes *narrative* sense, of a kind only the best of novelists are in command of, that he should discover his calling in life as a teacher and converter. Malcolm has his own theories for nearly everything that interests him—theories of language and etymology (he has an autodidact's sense of word-magic, dating from the time in prison when studying a dictionary, page by page, in a folklorish fury of self-improvement, began quite literally to give him an extravagant new intuition of power and freedom, as of one suddenly finding a key to his enemy's most treasured secrets); theories about how Socrates' wisdom came from initiation into the mysteries of black Egypt and about the persecuted black philosopher Spinoza and the black poet Homer, cognate with Omar and Moor, and about who really wrote Shakespeare and translated the English Bible (it was that subtle tyrant King James himself) and why. Of course we can laugh at a lot of this from the pewboxes of a more orderly education, but I find myself impressed even in these odd instances with the unfailing rationality of the uses to which Malcolm put his thought, the intelligence even here concerning what really matters to him—which is the meaning of his life as a black man in the United States and the enormous responsibilities of a position of authority and leadership in which he can count on no help from the official, institutionalized culture but what he wrenches out for himself.

But it is, again, the prodigy of his own conversion that gives him the most direct confirmation of his beliefs; the awareness of himself as a man capable of these transforming changes that gives him confidence in his testimony's importance, that lets him say, "Anything I do today, I regard as urgent." The *Autobiography* was written to serve at once a religious and a political cause, the cause of the religion of Islam and the cause of black freedom, and it is filled with the letter of Malcolm's teaching. In the later chapters especially, more and more of the text is portioned out to explanations of essential doctrine and to social and political commentary and analysis. But here, too, it is a personal authority that comes through to us and makes the difference. I should like to try to characterize this authority a little further. I first read Malcolm's autobiography when I happened also to be reading through the Pauline epistles in the New Testament; the chance result was a sharp consciousness of fundamental resemblances. Resemblances, I mean, to the voice and manner of the Paul who not only is teaching his people the law of the new faith (to which he himself is a latecomer, and by hard ways) but who suffuses his teaching with all the turbulence of his own history and masterful personality. Two recent students of Paul's letters, Charles Buck and Greer Taylor, have commented on the singularity of this element in Paul: "a presumption of personal authority on the part of the writer which is quite unlike that of any other New Testament author." Malcolm, too, writes as the leader of a new, precariously established faith, which he is concerned to stabilize against destructive inner dissensions yet without losing any of the priceless communal fervor and dedication that have been released by it. So at every point he brings to bear the full weight of his own reputation and active experience, including his earlier follies and excesses—precisely as Paul does in, for example, the astonishing final chapters of Second Corinthians, full as they are of the liveliest and most immediate self-reference.[4] The tangible genius of both Paul and Malcolm as writ-

---

[4] There are other parallels. Much of the time Paul is writing (as in Philippians and First Thessalonians) for the very particular purpose of freeing Christian worship from the so-called Judaizers; to ward off, that is, that one sectarian deviation within the practice of the new faith which was most likely to blight its true ecumenical growth. So Malcolm, with the fresh changes, the broadening, in his thought that took place in the last years of his life—changes crystallized by his characteristically intense and transforming response, traveling abroad, to the polyracial vision of the true Islam and the free cosmopolitan outlook of black Africa—was writing finally to free Islam in America from the constraining prejudices of Elijah Muhammad.

Malcolm himself refers to Paul in defining to himself the character of his experience. The violent circumstances of Paul's conversion deeply impressed him; he speaks of reading the account in Acts "over and over" in the Norfolk County Prison library.

ers is to bring the authority of living personality, and of self-mastery, into the arena of what is understood to be an argument of the utmost consequence; a matter of life and death for those who commit themselves to it.

Malcolm's concerns are of course civil and political as well as sectarian. In his last years he had become, and knew it, a national leader as important as Dr. King; a leader moreover who, as the atmosphere of the Washington march of August, 1963, gave way to the ghetto riots of the next summer, was trusted inside Harlem and its counterparts as the established black leadership no longer was. And the last academic point I want to make about the literary character of Malcolm's book is that in this regard, too, as a political statement, its form is recognizably "classic." The model it quite naturally conforms to is that of the Political Testament, the work in which some ruler or statesman sets down for the particular benefit of his people a summary of his own experience and wisdom and indicates the principles which are to guide those who succeed him. The historian Felix Gilbert has called attention to this rather special literary tradition in his study of the background of Washington's Farewell Address. It is necessarily, in the number of its members, a limited tradition; besides Washington's address Professor Gilbert mentions examples attributed to Richelieu, Colbert, the Dutch republican Jan de Witt, Robert Walpole, Peter the Great, and Frederick the Great, who wrote at least two of them. My argument is not that Malcolm was in any way guided by this grand precedent, merely that in serving all his book's purposes he substantially re-created it—which is of course what the work of literature we call "classic" does within the occasion it answers to.

With *The Armies of the Night* it is not necessary to go so far afield for critical justification. Norman Mailer's standing as a proper literary figure has been less and less in doubt in recent years, and this book's selection for national prizes and awards was surprisingly well received in all concerned quarters. In fact a lot of readers who had doggedly stuck by Mailer while he was producing one after another of the most compellingly unsatisfactory books being published in a mountingly unsatisfactory era fell on *Armies* with exaggerated noises of approval; there was off-putting talk about his finally proving his claim to be the "best writer in America," and so forth. Yet I think it is a masterly book according to its kind—and what I would especially call attention to is the way it grows into its power and eloquence (not transcending the occasion but responding to it, pursuing it, with an unstinting fullness of consideration) by adopting, or reinventing, a classic American literary mode: the exploratory personal testament in which the writer describes how he has turned his own life into a practical moral experiment and put it out at wager according to the chances, and against the odds, peculiar to the public character of his time and circumstance.

Some of our best-known secular autobiographies have made this their leading theme or action—Franklin's most famously, Lincoln Steffens's in more recent times—and much narrative fiction also builds on this format, which lies open to a lot of latter-day civil mythology about the response to vocation, the testing of virtue, and the like. But Thoreau's *Walden* is the formal precedent I was particularly reminded of in reading Mailer's book, neither of them being, strictly speaking, an autobiography but the testamentary description of an episode of such gathered intensity that the shape and logic of whole life-histories may fairly be inferred from it. *The Armies of the Night* was written out in a few weeks, as against the nine years' gestation and seven rewritings that produced the *Walden* we read, and it does not on the whole serve the writer's peculiar work of language-refreshment and generative sentence-making as well as Thoreau's did; yet whose writing does do that work in these days of (as Jean-Luc Godard has defined them) grave and progressive semantic loss? But I think it fairly compensates in its greater practical spaciousness and hospitality of reference, the common realistic abundance, so to speak, of its narrational vocabulary. On this rich ground another American forerunner it brings to mind is *Roughing It* (itself underrated, critically), a book that is also a pointedly personal and, though differently balanced, partly comic and partly tragic account of a great national *massenbewegung*.

In his earlier books some constant excess of personal insistence—willfulness, egotism, unregulated ambition—kept Mailer straining after more than he could satisfactorily deliver; more, it also seemed, than his found or improvised materials could intrinsically support. Yet the failures always seemed to be of execution rather than of imaginative purpose. He was a writer made as impatient by his own inventions as by everything else, in literature or out of it, that was offering itself for public acceptance; a writer growing more and more distrustful of the whole established occasion of literary making. He clung to the idea of The Novel as the great field of the fame he thirsted for and to the older idea of (as he still puts it in *Armies*, though with an ironic detachment) the writer's "responsibility to educate the nation," yet he seemed in the event to disbelieve in both the old novel and the old pedagogic rationale with an intensity that was sometimes the only halfway convincing sign of real originality, real seriousness. Critical reactions were fairly uniform in their disapproval. It was a reviewer's commonplace that Mailer belonged to publicity rather than to literature; that, as Benjamin De Mott put it, he was in hostage to the national cult of Success and the "belief in the sanctity of The Career," and that the "desire for triumph" was greater than any willingness to define an adequate cause to triumph in. Up through *An American Dream*, his last proper novel, these remained reasonable views. But one way of describing the formal strengthening and consolidation of Mailer's more recent books (I include *Cannibals and Christians* and that genuine tour de force, *Why Are We in Vietnam?*, but not those being done from the first on journalistic assignment), books that have turned one reviewer after another right around from head-shaking to sober respect and praise, is that his time's history has, to say the least, brutally overtaken his private will to power. Even more, it has given that will legitimacy, in the consciousness of readers, as a kind of counter-force. Anything less strenuous or more temperate and circumspect would seem pathetically inadequate. The writer who is not fuming in apprehension and willful resistance may be the writer who, incredibly, has not yet really heard the bad news.

The public life of the past decade has not only given Mailer subjects worthy of the most vehement ambition; it has had the effect also of justifying themes, attitudes, that earlier seemed freakish or fantastic. He has been saying for years that the great contemporary subject was totalitarianism. Now we are all saying that, or something like it, and feeling it with a paralyzing oppressiveness. His obsession, as it used to seem, with conflicts of power and brute force, with pitting himself against rivals (not just other writers but more ferocious antagonists like Sonny Liston, the Kennedys, Lyndon Johnson), with combat to the death against some vast imaginary Thing called various names but most ominously "cancer," no longer strikes us as ersatz Hemingwayism but as a kind of nervy common sense; and we read him now with all the interest a witness-bearer deserves whose obsessions have been borne out by the explosion of actual events.

The Armies of the Night is directly and continuously about that world of totalitarian civil power that in our lifetime has clamped down on every natural life-agency, every human usage and custom of existence; that power which, in Mailer's words, not only exploits the present but consumes the past and gives every promise of demolishing whole territories of the future. The book is also, not unrelatedly, about egotism and the anarchic aggression of the immitigably self-enclosed against civil propriety, decency, equity, responsibility. This is the broad link to Thoreau's book that particularly catches attention. For in both *Armies* and *Walden* the use of the writer's own self-projected image or self-conceit—in large part through comic exaggeration and a broad yet dead serious social mockery—is tactically central. (Mailer is not the first American literary talent to be accused of throwing itself away in egotistical rant: an aspect of Thoreau's writing, strong in the opening pages of *Walden* and even stronger in the first drafts, that not only Lowell but even Emerson perhaps never really saw beyond.) Each book is a very personal record, yet each appeals again and again to a broad common awareness of the curious rhythms, urgencies, constraints of the self's engagement with life; each thus forms an objective argument on the individual revolutionist's great question, "What therefore is to be done?" In *The Armies of the Night* egotism becomes not an instrument of self-promotion and performative self-betrayal but a theme for discourse, a controlled element in the essential structure. If you do not see this fairly soon, the first chapters of *Armies* can strike you as exhibitionistic in the extreme, and you may not get past them. For egotism, Mailer knows, is itself a main part of that field of force that constitutes totalitarianism's stranglehold on the technocratic-capitalist order; it is that arrogance of self that nourishes the arrogance of bureaucracies and of those nations we call advanced; it is also, ironically, a main source of the only really effective opposition to it. One way or another, it is the force we live by.

In *The Armies of the Night* the narrative dialectic between private and public motives, self-regard and national crisis, is rich and continuous, and it enters the book altogether naturally; for Mailer comes into the Pentagon march not simply as observer and chronicler but as a free participant. In the rites of gesture-making and the risks of real physical danger he is equal in status to everyone else. (This is the element necessarily missing, except by subrogation, in his reports on the 1968 conventions and the moon shot.) This ironic back-and-forth sustains, for example, the comedy of those opening chapters, indeed of the whole first part of the book, in which Mailer is trying to fit himself into the demonstration in a way that will satisfy all his motives, all the psychic and moral, not to speak of carnal, pressures operating within him and around him. The old quasi-religious theme, so peremptory in earlier American literature, that it is our deepest moral task to do nothing that is not in harmony with our whole creaturely being crisscrosses the equally grand theme that the struggle for civil justice must supersede all other vocations and responsibilities.[5] In the process the narrative becomes a very anatomy of "bad faith" (and re-

[5] I sometimes think that the deepest function of "literature"— which exists by way of a refusal to serve directly either the Platonic imperatives of justice or the eschatological imperatives of sanctification yet achieves wisdom and full efficacy only by recognizing in some way the immense overbearing reasonableness of both—is to bear witness to the impossibility of reconciling these tasks except existentially, in living out this essential irreconcilability and turning it into a governing condition and fact of exist-

stores some richness of meaning to this jaded modern concept): that faith-with-reasons, none of them quite pure at the best, which is all we can reasonably count on being gifted with in our trial of life.

Let me try to give a little of the common flavor of this narrative dialectic, which is the book's power coil and the means of releasing the strong prose hymn it closes with. The main narrative begins with a telephone call summoning Mailer to take part in the upcoming demonstration, one that is going to be "different," it is promised, from all previous ones, a real open-ended confrontation. Immediately the back-and-forth of indecision begins. Something is being asked that "would not be easy to refuse but would be expensive to perform." Is it a challenge that has come in fatal response to a growing private conviction that he is curdling, going soft or stale as a vital agent; that none of his chosen projects has yet "cost him enough"? The affair will be dangerous—and a little "bubble of fear tilts somewhere about the solar plexus" that will grow as the days and hours pass and in the event burst inside him like an uncontrollable abscess. Yet there are interesting tactical problems, the romantic appeal of deploying small forces to outmaneuver great ones, perhaps the chance to save the whole demonstration from its own virtuous ineptness. He hears that Paul Goodman and Dwight Macdonald will be on hand, and he smells out the sour atmosphere of the instinctive loser, which he hates (metaphors of smell and taste, palatal sourness and sweetness, are major in the book's rhetoric); but Bill Coffin

---

ence. (When we tire of the saints, Emerson remarked, Shakespeare is our city of refuge.)

Mailer's own use of "existential" has been famously loose, yet I think this is the occupational truth his behavior as a writer has pivoted on at its best.

with his Ivy League bark of authority sounds like a birthright winner and in Robert Lowell there is the truly rarified air of one casually above and beyond ignoble apprehensions of winning and losing. Mailer distrusts these "idiot mass manifestations"; he has, moreover, genuine doubts about the morality of selective draft resistance; his own instincts, he feels again, are "conservative and warlike"; yet at news that paratroopers are massing the old Wild Man rises within him, the one who once "at the edge of paralysis" stood up to challenge Sonny Liston face to face; and in the throes of the experience that his wager of participation opens to him—panic, arrest, a touch of manhandling, common imprisonment—the "nerve for adventure" that he has learned to trust as his truest literary resource, though it always gets him into trouble, asserts itself and takes command.

And there is also his career, his public image; he never ceases, in the "personal history" that forms the first three-quarters of the book, to be Norman Mailer the well-known writer, who must consider first of all whether this event really belongs to his own special obstacle-course of literary and moral fortune. Is marching about in ill-organized and dubiously effective mass demonstrations an appropriate action for a serious writer, especially a demonstration directed by the kind of undiscriminating liberal right-mindedness of which the first symptom is always soggy prose? On the other hand, can he get around the fact that there is never any graceful way of refusing the appeals of right-mindedness with a clear conscience? Well, then, why resist so remarkable a chance to try out his "existential" act before so intent an audience, to be Master of Ceremonies once more, to test himself on the latest front line of contemporary reality, even if it means, as increasingly it seems likely to, missing the party he is scheduled to attend in

New York that night? Yet suppose the event is not finally one he can absorb into his literary ecosystem? Suppose he is really changed by it—either profoundly violated, maybe killed, a victim if not of paratrooper ordnance then of the sheer banality of too much liberal virtue, or else forced to see that in the final cataclysm, of which this demonstration may only be a first skirmish, he will not be the romantic guerrilla leader and strategist of his dreams but expendable, as shorn a lamb as any other? Vanity plays its strong part; among other details it is suddenly revealed that a BBC television crew which he has consented to have undertake a documentary on him is following him into battle and will be there to film his final one-man assault on the military police lines. And Honor, too, as the world measures it; for in Lowell's company, in particular, he cannot put aside the primitive claims of competitive comradeship *and* the stirring thought that in crossing into Virginia in what may be the opening engagement in a long civil war he will be marching with the ghosts of the Union dead.

All this is in the long first part of the narrative. In the structure of the book it is the private matrix that will be gradually burned away as the full objective dimensions of the event are revealed. The overpublicized framework of speculation about the kinds of truth possible to novels and histories does not seem to me to have any great theoretical importance or interest, but it functions well as a scaffolding for the basic movement of the narrative, which is from pugnacious personal comedy to prophetic witness and litany, with "the Protagonist" (as Mailer calls himself) increasingly subordinated to the high historical occasion. Certain passages of objective action and movement—the first climax of the march over the bridge, the oddly relaxed night bus-ride to some obscure Virginia jail —are among the finest in the book; and at the end, in the moving evocation of the ordeal in the Washington jail of those Quakers whose resistance to totalitarian power becomes not just an afternoon's symbolic foray in front of television cameras but a life-and-death venture to the ragged edge of dehumanization and madness, Mailer is present only as an imaginative witness, asking unanswerable questions and offering his writer's metaphors of prayer and prophecy for those who have found a way through to the rare places of spirit that "no history can reach"; it is they who may just possibly be able, as no one else yet has, to break the lethal pattern of present history and forge a new human beginning. The great Blakean metaphors of parturition and ambiguous new birth with which the book ends are treacherous to reawaken—and I notice that that exceptionally sensible critic, Conor Cruse O'Brien, has described these last pages as "the kind of nonsense which can be perpetrated by excellent writers when they take to wallowing in their own idea of their own culture" [6]—but to my American ear they have the heart-sinking beauty of an entire fitness to this fearful, intimately American occasion; it is hard not to feel that they form a climax which has been fully earned.

Of course a judgment like that is itself in hostage to the public circumstance that engendered the book. It may well be that the power of statement I have felt in *The Armies of the Night* I will not feel a few years hence, if somehow we do get out of the Vietnam War and our own spreading civil crisis without some transmogrifying catastrophe. Even so, as a work of personal witness, I think the book will keep its interest and vitality. For of these two books, Malcolm's and Mailer's, I think this finally can be said: they give us what our major literary tradition—as we find it in Franklin, Emerson, Whit-

[6] *Albert Camus* (New York, 1970), p. 67n.

man, Melville, Henry James, Robinson, Fitzgerald, the Stevens of the *Letters*—has always propounded and celebrated at the core, and what, moreover, since Tocqueville has been defined as the blessing of life most imperiled by the characteristic development of a mass exploitative society; and that is the saving counterforce of personality. To borrow a couple of memorable cadences: in the midst of our immense depersonalization real personalities stand here, the indispensable mediators between consciousness and reality, between the life we still might learn to make and the life that bears down on us with the dead weight of all our past collusions. Real personalities—but of course only those who know the special impoverishment of life that comes with the loss of the poetry of human personality will know what it means for these two writers to have survived the violations of personal life and being our deadly era has made commonplace, and borne strong and truthful witness to them.

 THE ENGLISH INSTITUTE, 1970

Northrop Frye, *Massey College, University of Toronto*
James M. Osborn, *Yale University*
William K. Wimsatt, *Yale University*

ARCHIVIST

David V. Erdman, *State University of New York,*
  Stony Brook, and New York Public Library

 THE PROGRAM

TUESDAY, SEPTEMBER 8, THROUGH FRIDAY, SEPTEMBER 11, 1970

I. The Personal Mode in American Literature
   Directed by J. C. Levenson, University of Virginia

   Tues.   9:30 A.M.   Anne Bradstreet "Expos'd to Publick
                       View"
                       *Ellen Moers, Columbia University and
                       Barnard College*

   Tues. 11:00 A.M.   Franklin, Thoreau, Whitman, and Henry
                       Adams: Autobiography in America
                       James M. Cox, Dartmouth College

   Wed.   9:30 A.M.   Witness and Testament: Two
                       Contemporary Classics
                       Warner Berthoff, Harvard University

   Wed.   11:00 A.M.   The Negro Writer and the Political
                       Climate
                       *Saunders Redding, The George
                       Washington University*

II. Pastoral in the English Renaissance
    Directed by Paul J. Alpers, University of California, Berkeley

Tues.   1:45 P.M.   The Eclogue Tradition and the
                      Nature of Pastoral
                      Paul J. Alpers, University of California,
                      Berkeley
Tues.   3:15 P.M.   The King's Arcadia
                      Stephen Orgel, University of California,
                      Berkeley
Wed.   1:45 P.M.   Marvell and the Fictions of Pastoral
                      David Kalstone, Rutgers University
Wed.   3:15 P.M.   "Woods Worthy of a Consul":
                      Pastoral and the Sense of History
                      Michael J. K. O'Loughlin, Yale
                      University

III.   The Study of Narrative Techniques in Contemporary
        European and American Criticism
        Directed by Paul De Man,
        The Johns Hopkins University

Thurs.   9:30 A.M.   The Function of Indeterminacy in Prose
                      Fiction
                      Wolfgang Iser, Universität Konstanz
Thurs. 11:00 A.M.   The Irrelevant Detail and the
                      Emergence of Form
                      Martin Price, Yale University
Fri.   9:30 A.M.   Molestation and Authority in Narrative
                      Fiction
                      Edward W. Said, Columbia University
Fri.   11:00 A.M.   Historical and Narrative Time in Proust
                      Gérard Genette, École des hautes études,
                      Paris

IV.   Wordsworth
       Directed by Geoffrey Hartman, Yale University

Thurs.   1:45 P.M.   Wordsworth's Veiled Vision
                      Kenneth Johnston, Indiana University
Thurs.   3:15 P.M.   Wordsworth and the Music of Sound
                      John Hollander, Hunter College

| Fri. | 1:45 P.M. | Voices in the Open: Wordsworth, Eliot, and Stevens
Thomas R. Whitaker, University of Iowa |
| Fri. | 3:15 P.M. | Romantic Difference and Wordsworth's Poetic
Walter J. Ong, S.J., Saint Louis University |

REGISTRANTS, 1970

Ruth M. Adams, Wellesley College; Gellert S. Alleman, Rutgers University at Newark; Marcia Allentuck, City College, CUNY; Paul J. Alpers, University of California, Berkeley; Shahla Anand, Montclair State College; Judith Anderson, Cornell University; Valborg Anderson, Brooklyn College, CUNY; Stanford Apseloff, Kent State University

George W. Bahlke, Kirkland College; Charles W. Baird, Youngstown State University; Stewart A. Baker, Rice University; Rev. J. Robert Barth, s.j., Harvard University; Phyllis Bartlett, Queens College, CUNY; Adrianne Baytop, Douglass College, Rutgers University; Lester A. Beaurline, University of Virginia; John E. Becker, Fairleigh-Dickinson University; Maurice Beebe, Temple University; Alice R. Benson, Eastern Michigan University; Edward I. Berry, University of Virginia; Warner Berthoff, Harvard University; Larry Best, University of Connecticut; Sheila Blanchard, Northern Illinois University; Max Bluestone, University of Massachusetts at Boston; Charles R. Blyth, Brandeis University; Fredric V. Bogel, Connecticut College; Lynda D. W. Bogel, Yale University; Anne C. Bolgan, University of Western Ontario; Philip Bordinat, West Virginia University; John D. Boyd, s.j., Fordham University; Sister Ann Patrick Brady, Trinity College; Frank Brady, CUNY; Albert R. Braunmuller, Yale University;

Lee Bliss Braunmuller, University of California, Berkeley; James
H. Broderick, University of Massachusetts, at Boston; Mary Lynn
Broe, University of Connecticut; Reuben A. Brower, Harvard
University; Lawrence Buell, Oberlin College; Daniel W. Burke,
F.S.C., La Salle College; Morrill Burke, University of Maine at
Portland; Sister M. Vincentia Burns, O.P., Albertus Magnus Col-
lege; Lois Byrns, Stout State University

Ronald Campbell, Harcourt Brace Jovanovich, Inc.; Robert Cas-
erlo, Yale University; Sister Rita Margaret Chambers, O.P., Caldwell
College; Kent Christensen, Upsala College; Ralph A. Ciancio,
Skidmore College; A. R. Cirillo, Northwestern University; James
L. Clifford, Columbia University; James H. Coberly, George
Washington University; Richard Cody, Amherst College; Arthur
N. Collins, State University of New York at Albany; Rowland L.
Collins, University of Rochester; David B. Comer III, Georgia In-
stitute of Technology; Sister Marie Cornelia, Nazareth College of
Rochester; David Cowden, Swarthmore College; Rosemary Cow-
ler, Lake Forest College; James M. Cox, Dartmouth College; G.
Armour Craig, Amherst College; Robert True Crosman, Williams
College; Marion Cumpiano, University of Puerto Rico

Irene Dash, Columbia University; Jack Davis, University of Con-
necticut; Stuart A. Davis, Yale University; Winifred M. Davis,
Columbia University; Leonard W. Deen, Queens College, CUNY;
Paul De Man, The Johns Hopkins University; Constance Ayers
Denne, Baruch College, CUNY; C. J. Denne, Jr., College of New
Rochelle; Charlotte D'Evelyn, Mount Holyoke College; E. Talbot
Donaldson, Yale University; Sister Rose Bernard Donna, C.S.J.,
The College of Saint Rose; John H. Dorenkamp, Holy Cross Col-
lege; Dan Ducker, Millersville State College; Georgia Dunbar,
Hofstra University

Benjamin V. Early, Mary Washington College; Irvin Ehrenpreis,
University of Virginia; George P. Elliott, Syracuse University;
W. R. Elton, CUNY; Martha Winburn England, Queens College,
CUNY; David V. Erdman, State University of New York at
Stony Brook and New York Public Library; Andrew V. Ettin,
Cornell University; Johanna L. Ettin, Ithaca, New York; Sister
Marie Eugenie, I.H.M., Immaculata College

George S. Fayen, Smith College; Robert Folkenflik, University of Rochester; Leslie D. Foster, Northern Michigan University; Hans J. Freund, Union College; Barbara Friedberg, Columbia University; Albert B. Friedman, Claremont Graduate School; Northrop Frye, University of Toronto

Harry R. Garvin, Bucknell University; Jesse C. Gatlin, Jr., U.S. Air Force Academy; Marilyn Gaull, Temple University; Blanche H. Gelfant, State University of New York at Syracuse; Alexander Gelley, Cornell University; Gérard Genette, Ecole des hautes études, Paris; H. K. Girling, York University; Richard L. Goldfarb, York University; David J. Gordon, Hunter College, CUNY; Sister Mary Eugene Gotimer, College of Mount St. Vincent; Thomas M. Greene, Yale University; M. E. Grenander, State University of New York at Albany; John C. Guilds, University of South Carolina; Bradley Gunter, Boston College; Allen Guttmann, Amherst College

Vera Hackman, Elizabethtown College; Jean H. Hagstrum, Northwestern University; Lawrence S. Hall, Bowdoin College; Robert W. Hanning, Columbia University; Richard Harrier, New York University; Geoffrey Hartman, Yale University; Carol A. Hawkes, Finch College; A. W. Heidemann, Carleton University; Richard E. Henrich, Jr., New York University; James L. Hill, Michigan State University; Rev. William B. Hill, s.j., University of Scranton; C. Fenno Hoffman, Jr., Rhode Island School of Design; Daniel G. Hoffman, University of Pennsylvania; John Hollander, Hunter College, CUNY; Frank S. Hook, Lehigh University; Vivian C. Hopkins, State University of New York at Albany; Sheila Houle, Hampshire College; Clayton E. Hudnall, University of Hartford; John W. Huntington, Rutgers University; Samuel Hynes, Northwestern University

Wolfgang Iser, Universität Konstanz

E. D. H. Johnson, Princeton University; Richard A. Johnson, Mount Holyoke College; S. F. Johnson, Columbia University; Kenneth Johnston, Indiana University

Robert P. Kalmey, Shippensburg State College; David Kalstone, Rutgers University; Marjorie Kaufman, Mount Holyoke College;

Robert Kellogg, University of Virginia; Sister Eileen Kennedy, College of Saint Elizabeth; Veronica M. S. Kennedy, St. John's University; Joseph A. Kinney, Jr., Villanova University; Karl Kroeber, Columbia University

J. Craig La Driere, Harvard University; Robert Langbaum, University of Virginia; Jon S. Lawry, Westminster College; Eleanor Winsor Leach, Villanova University; Lewis Leary, University of North Carolina, Chapel Hill; J. C. Levenson, University of Virginia; Thomas S. W. Lewis, Skidmore College; George Lord, Yale University; Sister Alice Lubin, College of Saint Elizabeth; Eben W. Ludlow, Harcourt Brace Jovanovich

Isabel G. MacCaffrey, Tufts University; Patricia McFate, University of Illinois, Chicago; Nancy B. McGhee, Hampton Institute; T. J. McKenzie, U.S. Coast Guard Academy; Richard Macksey, The Johns Hopkins University; Cdr. J. B. Mahon, U.S. Coast Guard Academy; Irving Malin, City College, CUNY; Robert Marsh, University of Chicago; Sister Catherine Regina Marski, s.c., St. John's University; Louis Martz, Yale University: Donald C. Mell, Jr., University of Delaware; Michael J. Mendelsohn, U.S. Air Force Academy; J. Hillis Miller, The Johns Hopkins University; Ellen Moers, Columbia University and Barnard College; W. T. Moynihan, University of Connecticut; Thomas Mulvey, St. Francis College; Howard M. Munford, Middlebury College

Jack L. Nelson, Agnes Scott College; Lowry Nelson, Jr., Yale University; William Nelson, Columbia University; Ruby Nemser, Univrsity of British Columbia; Sister Macaria Neussendorfer, Yale University; Sister Ann Judith Newton, Trinity College; William T. Noon, s.j., Le Moyne College; Lawrence Noriega, Sweet Briar College

Eileen O'Gorman, Manhattanville College; Mrs. Richard Ohmann, Connecticut College; Michael J. K. O'Loughlin, Yale University; Walter J. Ong, s.j., Saint Louis University; Mother Thomas Aquinas O'Reilly, o.s.u., College of New Rochelle; Stephen Orgel, University of California, Berkeley; James M. Osborn, Yale University; Alicia Ostriker, Rutgers University; Charles A. Owen, Jr., University of Connecticut

Stephen M. Parrish, Cornell University; Harry Pauley, Shippensburg State College; Richard Pearce, Wheaton College; Roy Harvey Pearce, University of California, San Diego; Henry H. Peyton, III, Memphis State University; Barry Phillips, Wellesley College; E. L. Piepho, Sweet Briar College; Patricia G. Pinka, Agnes Scott College; Richard Poirier, Rutgers University; Sandra K. Pouchet, University of Connecticut; Anne L. Prescott, Barnard College; Robert O. Preyer, Brandeis University; Martin Price, Yale University; Theodore Price, Montclair State College; William H. Pritchard, Amherst College; Max Putzel, University of Connecticut; Bridget Puzon, o.s.u., Harvard University

Richard E. Quaintance, Jr., Rutgers University

Norman Rabkin, University of California, Berkeley; John Racin, West Virginia University: C. Earl Ramsey, Bryn Mawr College; Saunders Redding, The George Washington University; Compton Rees, University of Connecticut; Donald H. Reiman, Carl H. Pforzheimer Library; Joseph N. Riddel, State University of New York, Buffalo; John H. Robison, Michigan State University; Thomas P. Roche, Jr., Princeton University; Roger B. Rollin, Franklin and Marshall College; Beryl Rowland, York University; Rebecca D. Ruggles, Brooklyn College, CUNY; Philip C. Rule, s.j., University of Detroit

Edward W. Said, Columbia University; Phillips Salman, Cleveland State University; Florence R. Sandler, University of Puget Sound; Robert Sapora, University of Connecticut; Bernard N. Schilling, University of Rochester; Helene B. M. Schnabel, New York City; J. T. Schultz, Dartmouth College; Richard Sexton, Fordham University; F. Parvin Sharpless, Germantown Friends School; Frank C. Shuffelton, University of Rochester: Norman Silverstein, Queens College, CUNY; Lowell L. Simmons, Florida A. & M. University; Raman K. Singh, University of Virginia; Calvin Skaggs, Drew University; Sister Mary Francis Slattery, Mount Saint Vincent-on-Hudson; Barbara H. Smith, Bennington College; Thomas N. Smith, Simsbury, Connecticut; Nelle Smither, Douglass College; Susan Snyder, Swarthmore College; Ian Sowton, York University; Mark Spilka, Brown University; Holly Stevens, Yale

University; Keith Stewart, University of Cincinnati; Donald R. Stoddard, Skidmore College; Albert E. Stone, Emory University; R. F. Storch, Tufts University; Jean Sudrann, Mount Holyoke College; Maureen Sullivan, University of Pennsylvania; Joseph H. Summers, University of Rochester; U. T. Miller Summers, Rochester Institute of Technology; Donald R. Swanson, Upsala College

John Taylor, Universty of Chicago; Nathaniel Teich, University of Oregon; Margret G. Trotter, Agnes Scott College

Virginia Walker Valentine, University of South Florida; Ruth M. Vande Kieft, Queens College, CUNY; John B. Van Sickle, University of Pennsylvania; Helen Vendler, Boston University

Willis Wager, Boston University; Eugene M. Waith, Yale University; Andrew J. Walker, Georgia Institute of Technology; Emily Wallace, Swarthmore College; Howard Waskow, Reed College; Ronald A. Wells, U.S. Coast Guard Academy; Christian S. Wenger, Elizabethtown College; Thomas R. Whitaker, University of Iowa; Joseph Wiesenfarth, University of Wisconsin; Maurita Willett, University of Illinois; Marilyn L. Williamson, Oakland University; Dorothy M. Willis, New Haven, Connecticut; Jack H. Wilson, Old Dominion University; W. K. Wimsatt, Yale University; Calhoun Winton, University of South Carolina; Carl Woodring, Columbia University; Robert D. Wyatt, Drexel University

Donez Xiques, Villa Maria Academy

James Dean Young, Georgia Institute of Technology

Steven N. Zwicker, Washington University

42130